A TIME
FOR
REFLECTION

A TIME
FOR
REFLECTION
from the
SPOKEN WORD

given by
J. Spencer Kinard

Deseret Book Company
Salt Lake City, Utah

©1986 Bonneville Media Communications
All rights reserved
Printed in the United States of America

No part of this book may be reproduced in any
form or by any means without permission in writing
from Bonneville Media Communications,
130 Social Hall Avenue, Salt Lake City, Utah 84111.

ISBN 0-87579-049-6
Library of Congress Catalog Card Number 86-71701

First printing September 1986
Second printing December 1986
Third printing March 1988
Fourth printing December 1988
Fifth printing September 1989

Published by Deseret Book Company,
P.O. Box 30178, Salt Lake City, Utah 84130

Contents

EDUCATION 167

SELF-WORTH 175

Acknowledgments

My grateful acknowledgment and thanks for the contributions of Maurine Ward, Duane Hiatt, Michael Robinson, Clifton Jolley and Ray Haeckel, without whose assistance this book would not have been possible.

ENJOYING
LIFE

A Quiet, Sunny Day

To sit on a grassy hillside bathed in warm sunlight on a quiet, windless day is one of life's simple pleasures. The calm of the moment brings a peaceful reassurance to the soul and makes us wonder why life can't always be like that. Likewise, perhaps we've witnessed the glassy, smooth surface of a lake at sunset and compared that to the wind-tossed waves of a stormy day. "Why?" we wonder. "Why must we have the storms?"

The answer, to those who think about it, is simple: it is nature's way. It is the self-renewing process by which one thing creates another thing. Without the rains and snows of winter, the rivers would soon be dry, and the lake shores would begin to recede. And so we learn to take precautions from the storm so we can return on a sunny day to enjoy what the storm helped create.

Sometimes that which seems most destructive in nature can be of great benefit. On the prairie lands of the arid western United States grow delicate grasses and flowers that provide forage for the wild and domestic herds that roam the land. In time, the grasses are challenged for survival by the stronger and bigger sagebrush and tamarack trees. But then nature sends what seems to be a destructive fire that blackens the land. With a little help from mankind to prevent erosion, the grasses return more numerous than ever, and soon the prairie is more lush and green than before.

Our lives face similar challenges and opportunities. The physical, emotional, and spiritual storms that regularly engulf us are part of the self-renewing, learning process that keeps us on the road of eternal progression. Like nature, such storms help clear away the debris that clutter our lives. They prepare us to move forward in personal development. They help open our eyes to new insights and understanding. And they teach us to take precautions so other storms don't destroy us.

Yes, we all seek for quiet, happy days of contentment. But we must also learn to understand that the storms along the way will make the sunny days—whenever they come—more beautiful.

Live for Today

Those who have some clue that they are approaching death—the aged, the terminally ill—seem to gain an insight into the meaning of life. Their conclusion is universal: Live life to the fullest; live life as if each day were the last, as well it may be. This is a motto to measure life not by its length but by its depth.

To live is not merely to breathe; it is to experience, to make use of our senses, our capacity to feel. To be alive merely to acquire material possessions or fame, or to experience only sensual pleasure, is to trade our irreplaceable time for that which is worthless. Too soon life is gone. Even as we speak, a portion of it has fled. Regardless of its length, life is short. The man who dies at 100 and the man who dies at 20 lose one and the same thing: the opportunity to live for today.

"Had I the chance to live life over," wrote Michael Robinson in *The Existential Voyage,* "I would do things somewhat differently. I would understand at the beginning that much of our life is spent in vain pursuits. If I could do it again, I would hate less and love more, work less overtime and spend more time with my family, argue less and listen more, collect fewer debts and more friends.

"If God granted me a second chance, I would grow closer to living things—to petunias, to aspen trees, to kittens, to my children. Bedtime stories would be as important as news stories; valentines and birthdays would be as honored as paydays. I would never go to bed without saying to someone, 'I love you,' or without experiencing the beauty of a song, a poem, or a painting.

"And finally, each morning as I arose I would repeat these words: The past is gone and tomorrow may never come . . . I will live for today."

Simplicity

Henry David Thoreau once observed that our lives are often frittered away by detail. He advised us to simplify! Simplify!

There is great strength in making our lives and habits lean and trim. It will bring us needed strength to survive the growing complexity of our day and age. Too many of us overload ourselves with "extra baggage," and then wonder why we lead quiet lives of desperation. We who could choose simplicity choose complexity.

Learning how little rather than how much we can get along with will help us develop inner and outer harmony. It doesn't take long to learn what extraordinary spiritual freedom and peace such simplification and harmony can bring. Even in spiritual matters, we can find strength in simplicity. Recall how simple and direct God's commandments are: Thou shalt love the Lord thy God; love thy neighbor; thou shalt not kill, nor steal. These rules are not complicated. And all who wish may understand them and obey them. But, even in biblical times, there was a natural tendency to complicate life and thereby excuse oneself from God's laws.

In *Things As They Really Are,* Neal Maxwell wrote, "We like intellectual embroidery. We like complexity because it gives us an excuse for failure . . . [It provides] more and more refuges for those who don't want to comply; . . . thereby [increasing] the number of excuses people can make for failure to comply."

Simplicity should be a universal goal—not only for all people, but in all aspects of our lives. It means seeing every day as it is, not idly dreaming about what we hope it would be. It means finding peace of mind within us, not on a sunny make-believe island in the South Pacific. Happiness does not come through material prosperity and instant gratification, even though we live in a society of "buy now, pay later." The more we pamper our desires and let them rule us, the more they will demand.

It is better to focus on simple thoughts, simple needs, simple pleasures and simple guidelines for life, rather than carry the heavy yoke of a cluttered existence. We would all do better to make simplicity a state of life and mind so we can retain a true awareness of both spiritual and temporal matters.

Things

In a world where most of us are bombarded with thousands of commercial messages each year, we may begin to think the highest purpose for our existence is to consume. After all, we've been reminded of the many ways we can smell sweeter, drive faster, eat more conveniently, relax on newer furniture, and save more money by spending it now. Some of us have learned to believe that what we have is never enough; and in an economy where so many pocketbooks are growing thinner, the resulting tension between what we think we need and what we can afford may result in unhappiness.

But Benjamin Franklin said, "There are two ways of being happy: We may either diminish our wants or augment our means—either will do—the result is the same; and it is for each man to decide for himself, and do that which happens to be the easiest. If you are idle or sick or poor, however hard it may be to diminish your wants, it will be harder to augment your means. If you are active and prosperous or young or in good health, it may be easier for you to augment your means than to diminish your wants. But if you are wise, you will do both at the same time, young or old, rich or poor, sick or well; and if you are very wise you will do both in such a way as to augment the general happiness of society."

Now those who seek to augment their means will find it to be an individual journey, each path different according to a person's talent, opportunities, and energy. But there are some similarities for all of us in learning to diminish our wants. We need to understand that diminished wants do not make a diminished life. Wanting less may not lower our standard of living, but actually increase it.

Too many of us focus our existence on earning, acquiring, spending, and consuming. We use up our time getting things and then maintaining them, finding a place to store them, fixing them when they break down, guarding them against theft, and then upgrading them when a newer model comes out. Stuff . . . is that the measure of life, letting stuff fill up our hours and then our hearts?

Perhaps instead we should be like the man who said he had more than Carnegie or Rockefeller. "How's that?" asked a friend. "Because I have all I need, and they always wanted more," he answered. Let us simplify our wants and then our lives, throwing open the windows of our souls to let a clean, sweet breeze flow through. Let us learn to evaluate under a stricter standard what we think we need. Will this really enhance my life? Is it worth the financial tension it will cause? Can I do without it?

None of us really want to spend our precious hours on earth primarily on things that will yellow, age, break down, or end up in the city garbage. We only pass this way once, and there are finer things to do.

The Priceless Value of Common Things

Some of the things we value most in life—though we might not always realize it—are the most common. This fact prompted one author to observe, "Genius is recognizing the uniqueness in the unimpressive. It is looking at a homely caterpillar, an ordinary egg and a selfish infant, and seeing a butterfly, an eagle and a saint." Well, that may be the essence of genius, and if it is, then we were all born with a bit of genius. It is the natural curiosity and imagination that makes a child stare at a bug or watch the clouds drift by—little touches that are common to us all when we're young. Unfortunately, as we grow older, our world usually becomes more complicated, and in the process we lose sight of some of life's most valuable and lovely things.

Artists, poets, composers, and other creative people make a life-style of digging deeper into the sights and sounds that most of us pass over as being too common to concern us. Robert Louis

Stevenson wrote in *Weir of Hermiston* that "the commonplaces are the great poetic truths." And poet Robert Frost wrote of birch trees bending or of a quiet fork in the forest road and drew from them marvelous symbolism and messages for mankind. Each of us can partake of these creative experiences if we will sensitize our spirits to the goodness and beauty in the world about us.

Perhaps in no area of our lives do we need this appreciation for the common things as much as we do in our relationships with each other. Often the common things people do are what make people uncommon, special, caring, and appreciated. Their common care and concern for everyone makes them uncommon.

And so, for those who have eyes to see, ears to hear, and hearts to feel, the common things and so-called common people of this world are in reality a multitude of little miracles waiting for us to discover such discoveries that might be of greatest value and bring us the greatest peace.

Shedding

Wherever did modern man get the idea that more was better? Unhappy is the corporate executive who cannot report that his company grew bigger during the year. Chambers of commerce urge their towns to constant growth. And individually, we hurry to acquire more and more possessions, to cram more and more into each day, until our lives become like stuffed suitcases that cannot close and that bulge and break with their loads.

Well, in every life there is much to do, a thousand fronts to respond to, distractions like mosquitos that nip at us from every side. There are, after all, responsibilities to carry at work, bills to pay, a household gadget to fix, the telephone to answer, the child's problem to solve, the appointment to keep, the meeting to attend. Too many voices at once to answer. And like practiced jugglers, we are supposed to perform all these demands skillfully. But even if we seem to do well at our myriad duties, they take their toll upon our inner lives.

We are fragmented, pulled apart, each demand exacting a little piece of us until there is no still point in our turning world.

We lose our central core, our inner harmony, feeling only as if we were a mass of hurriedly performed functions. If we are to ever again be whole, we must follow the advice of wise men through all the ages of time, and that is to seek not more in our lives but less. Not to add and add but to simplify. We lose touch with the springs that nourish us when we are encumbered with too many distractions, too many possessions. Simplify. Shed the impediments that cloud our vision.

At first, that may sound impossible. We cannot shed our jobs or subtract a child from our family; but there are things, less important things, we can shed. We can shed our false pride, which leads us to own more than we need, perhaps only to impress others. We can shed our performance in certain capacities that mean nothing to us. We can shed meaningless regret for past failures over which we no longer have control and that no longer matter. We can shed guilt over the unfinished task. We can shed anxiety for tomorrow's responsibility. Tomorrow is not yet upon us. We can shed physical possessions that break and need maintenance and do not add as much as they take from us. We can shed activities that do not enrich us, but merely numb our senses.

Despite so many marvelous public relations campaigns, more is not better. A full life is often a simple one, where there is room for purity of intention, singleness of purpose, and a settled heart.

HAPPINESS

Religion Brings Happiness

It is traditional to look upon the new year as a time to begin anew, to rise above past mistakes. It is also a time when many individuals examine their priorities and lifetime objectives and feel the need to increase their spirituality and religious commitment.

There is a strong relationship between happiness and certain religious values, such as the feeling that life has meaning and direction. Those who lack meaning in their lives tend to be less happy with almost every aspect of living—less satisfied with the recognition they receive, with their financial situation, with their home, job, marriage, friends, and community, and even with their own physical attractiveness.

On the other hand, people who feel in harmony with the universe and have confidence in their own guiding values tend to be somewhat better off than the rest of the population. Their health is better, and they report less anxiety, tiredness, and loneliness. People who have a strong sense that their lives have meaning and direction tend to be happier with the role religion plays in their lives, and they believe religion is important to their happiness.

True happiness is a state of the spirit, an attitude of the mind. It is not an external condition brought about by material things. The Savior told us that the spiritual road—the road to self-mastery—is the only road to true happiness.

There is an upswing in religious interest by young people, and the trend is especially strong among young adults, particularly those in their twenties and thirties. Religious leaders believe this movement is prompted, in part, by economic conditions, a sense of world crises, and a quest for an alternative to secular life-styles of the past few years. These young adults are finding a renewed strength and perspective that seem to help them in their personal lives. They are realizing that a relationship with God is an essential element in maintaining personal balance.

And so it is for each of us. The choice—whether to increase our religious commitment or not—is ours. And once made, it must be reaffirmed every day and every moment. It is hard to give up old habits and more difficult still to conquer our own wills. But the Lord will bless us in our efforts. He asks only that we have faith in him and make every effort to keep his commandments, which have been given to us for our own well-being and for our own lasting happiness.

Joy of Man's Desiring

"Jesu, Joy of Man's Desiring," a beautiful work by Bach, is one of the most beloved pieces in the literature of great music. It is so partly for its moving melody and because it captures and encompasses a thought and a hope that every human heart warms to: the pursuit of joy.

At first glance one might wonder how the life of Jesus could serve as a model in the search for joy. Jesus was born in the humblest of circumstances, resident of a tiny town in the backwaters of a captive nation. He was despised and rejected as "a man of sorrows, and acquainted with grief." (Isa. 53:3.) His attempts to preach love and caring to his people were cut short in the cruelest manner that men could devise.

So where was the joy in Jesus' life? By traditional measurements he had difficulty finding success in his work. He did not convert vast multitudes. But then, he did not measure his success in quantities. He was concerned with the quality of light and truth he might bring to even a single soul.

And did he enjoy the things of this world? No. He gained no

worldly wealth. But he did love the beautiful gifts of the earth. "Consider the lilies of the field," he said. "They toil not, neither do they spin: and yet I say unto you, That even Solomon in all his glory was not arrayed like one of these." (Matt. 6:28-29.)

He did not feel the joy of friendship. Though people flocked to hear him at times, they were equally willing to abandon him. In his darkest hour he was completely alone. Yet he enjoyed a friendship that would never fail, a friendship with his Father in Heaven. And this celestially centered joy sustained him through his trials.

And what of the joy of freedom? Bound, beaten, imprisoned, and finally crucified, he would appear to be a man of miseries, another of the world's sad captives at the mercy of the merciless. But in reality he was the freest of all because he had the power to impose his will on others, yet he chose not to.

And thus on closer inspection it would appear that Jesus was a man of joy, of the deepest, most permanent kind of joy. And in our own lives, as we fluctuate from frustration to fulfillment, pleasure to pain, we would do well to develop the deeper joys that he knew—joys like the calm waters of the ocean depths that pass unperturbed beneath the surface storms raging above them.

Anxious Living

"There is such a thing as taking ourselves and the world too seriously, or at any rate too anxiously," observed Henry Van Dyke. The song says, "We find them happy which endure in patience." Yet enduring to the end gives us a lot of worry. It seems, in fact, that worry is one of the great human pastimes. Indeed, we hardly consider ourselves fully responsible if we aren't worried about something. There is the constant anxiety about our performance, if we can measure up in what sometimes seems like an endless contest.

Now some believe there is a majesty in misery, a nobility in worry, thinking it is God's best way of disciplining his children. The question for us is, "Is that really so?" It was R.W. Dale who said, "We do not please God more by eating bitter ales than by eating honey. A cloudy, foggy, rainy day is not more heavenly than a day of sunshine. A funeral march is not so much like the music of angels as the songs of birds on a May morning. There is no more religion in the gaunt, naked forest in winter than in the laughing blossoms of the spring and the rich, ripe fruits of autumn."

Why do we get gloominess mixed up with glory, thinking that endless fussing and anxiety add to our performance? It is not the Lord's doing. The image of the gloomy Christian has been with us too long. The idea of the stressful soul being the only successful soul has deceived us.

The Lord is not the one who introduced woe into the world. It came from another author. God is purity and light, often the only source of sweetness in a world that seems too bitter for us. When He asks us to endure, it is to give us the courage against caving in to unhappiness. Even the natural world reflects his goodness. When the January world is an unrelenting gray, the bulbs of spring are already preparing to send forth their blossoms. Even when the sun is about to leave us in the evening, it does so in a dazzle of color.

So if life seems anxious and serious, it may be that we, ourselves, are taking it too anxiously, too seriously in some vain effort to be better or to please the Lord. We are fooled if we look for God's hand only in the lightning and not in the sunlight. If we miss happiness along the way, we've missed it all.

The Me Society

Critics call our modern world a "me society" in which everyone is trying desperately to please himself. We are taught to see people only in terms of "making it." The unsaid question that lurks behind every activity in this type of society is "Does this enhance me?" In fact, we've come to honestly believe that if we try hard enough, and long enough, and ambitiously enough to please ourselves—we finally will.

There is nothing wrong, of course, with desiring to be happy. There is an innate yearning in our nature to that very end. Where we seem to be so mistaken these days, however, is in believing that happiness is an end in itself and not a by-product of something else. We may satisfy all our senses and still not be satisfied. We may fulfill every selfish whim, aggrandize ourselves until our ego is the biggest thing in the world—and still feel empty. Many may have seen the world, but in its far-flung countries, they have still seen only themselves.

If happiness is not a product we can possess by pleasing ourselves, what is it a by-product of? Robert Browning once said, "Oh, make us happy and you make us good." That is certainly true, but so is its reverse. "Oh, make us good and you make us happy." Another writer, Horace Mann, observed, "In vain do they talk of happiness who never subdued an impulse in obedience to a principle. He who never sacrificed a present to a future good, or a personal to a general one, can speak of happiness only as the blind do of colors."

Because we are really children of God and our natures have the capacity to be as his, it will always go against the grain of reality to try to find happiness in self-indulgence instead of in self-mastery, in admiring those who are served instead of those who serve. The Lord has informed us of eternal laws and begged us to conform to them, not because he likes to see us struggle with principles that are above us, but because it is only in that struggle and triumph in them that happiness can ever be found.

When we seek for happiness elsewhere, in the satiating of our senses or the thrill of a moment, we are as children in an amusement park attracted by the bright lights and noisy promise of a temporary but false happiness. The problem with a "me society" and its pursuit of pleasure is simply that it does not work.

The Happiness of God

Happiness—a universal goal. But perhaps some of us have a hard time remembering when we were really happy, remembering when we laughed for the sheer joy of living. Some of us have perhaps looked at the apparent happiness of people who do not live virtuously, who are less than honest, who live only for today;

and we have mistakenly assumed that happiness is in some way attached to sin. Nothing could be further from the truth, although even the prophet Jeremiah was moved to ask God: "Wherefore doth the way of the wicked prosper? wherefore are all they happy that deal very treacherously?" (Jer. 12:1.) The answer the Lord gave him is that the happiness of sin is momentary and empty; and for that reason it is completely unlike the full and enduring happiness of righteousness, the happiness of God.

Nevertheless, we live in a world that has a misdirected devotion to happiness, that has turned happiness into a cult obsession. Many people have devoted themselves to a quest for personal fulfillment, have invested their lives in leisure and self-indulgence. And as they have done so, they have, as Jeremiah said they would, found themselves curiously unfulfilled, dissatisfied with their lives, and bored with living.

But simply because those who seek only happiness do not find it does not mean that God does not wish us to be happy. "Happy is that people," wrote the psalmist, "yea, happy is that people, whose God is the Lord." (Ps. 144:15.) The gospel of Jesus Christ is by definition the "good news" designed to make us happy, ordained to fulfill our lives and to teach us the happiness of virtuous living. And we discover through it that the love and dignity the gospel teaches are the only approach to true and enduring happiness.

God's happiness frequently requires sacrifice, always requires service. But it is the only happiness that will not leave us lonely once achieved, will not desert us in the hours of our greatest need. We love God and serve our fellowman so that we may be happy, so that, in the words of the psalmist, we may "make a joyful noise unto the Lord" and "serve [him] with gladness." (Ps. 100:1-2.)

Happiness—No Big Thing

The *U.S. News & World Report* noted that the question most people once evaluated themselves by was "Am I doing right?" Then that question was replaced with "Am I getting ahead?" But today many of us hear from a slightly tinny inner voice, "Am I having fun?"

Well, there's nothing wrong with the pursuit of happiness. It was even cited as an inalienable right in the Declaration of Independence. But we do have to worry when we realize that for too many that pursuit is a tiring and empty one. Some of us lie awake at night or plod through our daily routines always wondering, "When is it my turn?" We hope we'll be happy when a certain pressure has eased, when the bills are paid, when we get organized, when we get a promotion, when we finally have something to look forward to. And then the anticipated event occurs, and we still say plaintively with Walt Whitman, "Where is what I started for so long ago? And why is it yet unfound?"

If it is not found, perhaps we have been searching in the wrong place. Happiness is not a roller coaster moment, a giddy laugh, a constant good time. It is not even a supreme ecstatic hour, a dramatic high. It is the art of learning to celebrate life's small gifts, of making much of little things. Happiness is not tomorrow's promise. It is in this minute or not at all.

A newspaper editorial once observed that, "There is an evident effort in nature to be happy. Everything blossoms to express beauty, as well as lead to fruitage. Even the inorganic fashions itself into crystals, that absorb and flash back the sunlight. . . . Man has no right to be an exception—the only pessimist in the universe." We should avoid being that pessimist. We shouldn't expect happiness to be what it cannot be—a constant exhilaration.

If our morning is greeted with the sunshine jiggling through our curtains, then that's enough gift for today. If we catch the fragrance of orange blossoms, if a stranger does something nice, or if a child makes us laugh, then that's enough gift for today. Small things, everyday gifts have the power to make every day happy. When we stop scrutinizing ourselves to see if the world is making us properly glad, our eyes are suddenly free to see a thousand other beauties, to see the joy in the morning. That's enough gift for today.

SUCCESS

True Success

The definition of the word *success* varies from individual to individual, from culture to culture. For some people, it has to do with the acquisition of wealth. For others, success involves professional titles or social status. And still others define success in terms of the amount of time available for recreation or leisure. However, an entry from the diary of one American writer, M. L. Robinson, suggests that true success has more to do with the inner successes of the soul than with external prosperity: "I have never made more than enough money to buy the necessities of life; my works are largely unknown; except for the love of my family and a few good friends, I have earned no prestigious titles. But, I have lived simply, laughed frequently, and loved deeply—I am a success."

These words are food for thought: To live simply is to bring life into focus; it is to set priorities in life, rejecting the extravagant and the unnecessary while making room for the truly important. To live simply is to succeed at the organization of things for the sake of the soul. Laughter, another indication of true success according to Mr. Robinson, is an assurance of inner peace, a sign that all is well behind the partitioned walls of self. With laughter, even the poorest individual is a success; without it, the richest is a failure. Perhaps the greatest evidence of inner success is a sincere and profound affection for someone other than ourselves. Loving deeply implies a denial of our own wants in favor of the needs of others. Whether it is extended to wife, or to husband, or to children or grandparents, or to God, love is one of the soul's greatest accomplishments.

Jesus was the one who distinguished between the true success of the soul and the false achievements of fame and fortune: "For what shall it profit a man," he queried, "if he shall gain the whole world, and lose his own soul?" (Mark 8:36.) Indeed, of what value are the extrinsic possessions of wealth and notoriety without the internal prosperity that results from the personal achievements of the soul? With all of our successes, let us also achieve true success—the kind that comes from living simply, laughing frequently, and loving deeply.

The Faithful Heart

The women of the Choir have sung of hearts ever faithful and uncomplaining. Such hearts pump the lifeblood of the human race—they belong to the solid, steady, dependable and dutiful people who carry out their daily labors whether or not they feel like doing the work. Such people are the unsung heroes in every field of endeavor—the real professionals. Sidney Harris once observed that the difference between an amateur and a true professional is not that one is so stunningly superior in a single performance, but that one, because of determination, skill, and training, can perform well consistently, faithfully, time after time.

Such a man was Lou Gehrig, the great first baseman for the New York Yankees. Forty years ago, he set a record that has never been equalled and probably never will be. For fourteen years and more than 2,000 games, nothing kept him out of his uniform— not broken fingers and ribs, colds, flu, lumbago, headaches, pulled hamstrings, or sprained ankles. Late in his career, the team doctor X-rayed his hands and found seventeen broken bones that had healed themselves as Lou Gehrig ignored them and he played on.

Faithfulness and dependability are not spectacular, applause-winning virtues, but they are the foundation of any enduring accomplishment. How can we develop this dependability if we don't have it? Most of us have days when we feel like we could conquer the world and others when the weight of our work or even play seems almost more than we can carry. How can we smooth out these cycles and avoid getting giddy from our successes or morose about our problems? An old Rabbi offered this advice, "Every man should keep a message in each pocket written on a piece of paper. In times of self-satisfaction and complacency he should take out the one which reads, 'I am dust and ashes.' But when he is dejected and dispirited, he should take out the other and read, 'For my sake was the World created.' And at all times he should remember, I am made from the dust, but it is in God's image that I am made. I am God's creature, one of two thousand millions living upon the earth, yet even the hairs of my head are numbered."

This kind of balanced perspective can help us gain the dependability to get through the darkness to the dawn; to steadfastly place one foot before the other, no matter how difficult the terrain or how slow our progress; and to remember that no matter how dark the descent, there is light at the end of life's tunnel. It is the promise of the Lord, "He that shall endure to the end, the same shall be saved." (Mark 13:13.)

A Trio of Truths

Moral courage characterizes the highest order of manhood and womanhood. It is the courage to seek and to speak the truth; the courage to be just, to be honest, to resist temptation; the courage to do one's duty. A great deal of the unhappiness and much of the vice in the world come from a lack of moral courage and purpose. The weak and undisciplined person is at the mercy of every temptation. A national researcher studying self-fulfillment reported in *Time* that "nothing has subverted self-fulfillment more thoroughly than self-indulgence." In order to have moral courage and do the things that are best for us, we must believe we are capable—we must have faith in ourselves, as well as in our values. If we excuse ourselves because "we can't," we never will . . . for "without faith [we] can do nothing." (D&C 8:10.)

Popular cliches often miss the point of moral courage. For example, consider the description of a person groping for life as someone who "has not found himself." The statement is not accurate because self is created, not found. We change our circumstances by changing our attitudes and exercising our moral courage. Or consider those who give up on life and dismiss it as hopeless. They have become discouraged and have lost all hope. Of course, the Lord could intervene and help at any time, but he knows it is through the exercise of faith and courage that we grow and become stronger. We learn the virtue of self-discipline that helps forge strong character traits. And the cycle repeats itself again and again. By blending courage with faith, we create character. Character, in turn, brings the moral courage and faith to stand firm or yield when desirable. And so the circle—the trio of truths: courage, faith, and character—is complete, ready to begin again.

The actual building of moral courage is an individual, personal endeavor that goes on inside of us each day. It is an achievement, not a gift. It develops gradually through continuous right decisions, and it must be pursued systematically through the end of our days. Moral courage brings self-discipline, self-respect, and self-control. It brings victory over one's self, and that is the ultimate challenge facing each of us in the personal search for truth.

The Success of Failure

To some extent, what Charles Dickens concluded about his time in the *Tale of Two Cities* is also true about the present age. These days too may be construed by some to be "the best of times" and "the worst of times." Obviously, the degree of misfortune among our populace does not match the adversity of times past. Starvation and extreme poverty, at least in this country, are relatively unknown.

In an economic sense, though, many individuals are experiencing difficult times. In the face of apparent prosperity, hundreds of small businesses have had to close their doors during the last year or two. Large corporations are also having their share of problems; layoffs and production slowdowns are becoming commonplace. And a large percentage of individual wage earners, especially those who support families, are having a burdensome time making ends meet.

Through all of this, we are not to despair or become overly discouraged. Difficulties, and even failures, are only disheartening when they are viewed as ends in themselves. But when they are seen as they are, as means toward other successes, they then become opportunities. "We mount to heaven mostly on the ruins of our cherished schemes, finding our failures were successes," wrote A. B. Alcott. To this Keats added, "Failure is . . . the highway to success, inasmuch as every discovery of what is false leads us to seek earnestly after what is true, and every fresh experience points out some form of error which we shall afterward carefully avoid."

Adversity is the stepping stone to success. Continuous prosperity without the strengthening force of opposition breeds complacency and softness. Through adversity, new talents are discovered, talents that may have lain dormant otherwise. Adversity and economic stress are also the parents of invention. We invent substitutes for what we cannot afford. No doubt, the declining reservoir of fossil fuels will produce numerous and more efficient alternatives.

Yes, prosperity teaches, but the greater teacher is adversity. Through her we learn prudence and frugality; through her we learn to value what cannot be bought. In bracing ourselves against the strong winds of adversity we develop a greatness of soul that cannot be secured through entire lifetimes of success and prosperity.

The Need for Self-Discipline

In the Bible, praise is given not to the strong man who "taketh a city," but to the stronger man who "ruleth his spirit." (Prov. 16:32.) The stronger man—it is he who exercises constant control over his thoughts, his speech, and his actions. We call it *self-discipline.*

Many benefits come from self-discipline. It is essential if we are to renew ourselves, to become aware of the full range of our abilities. Seneca said, "Most powerful is he who has himself in his power." It takes self-discipline to understand ourselves, to know who we are, to live with ourselves. But as Josh Billings said in *Self-Renewal*, "It is not only the most difficult thing to know oneself, but the most inconvenient one, too." Is it any wonder then that by middle life many persons are accomplished fugitives from themselves?

But to know ourselves—to discover the virtues of self-control—will return benefits not only to us but to those around us as well. A successful family relationship demands self-discipline . . . from all its members—not just some. Without the give and take self-control allows, many family relationships would be harmed. Even from a historical perspective, the majority of desires and appetites that have degraded society would have shrunk into insignificance if there had been self-discipline, self-respect, and self-control.

Yes, victory over oneself—that is the ultimate challenge, the gateway to our greatest opportunities: to be one person, singular in word and deed. All virtues depend on self-discipline. It is the primary essence of character. Without discipline, our lives have no order. As Frederick Perthes said, "The government of one's self is the only true freedom for the individual." The most self-reliant, self-governing man is always under discipline. That is what gives him the power to follow his convictions and better prepare himself to face the trials of life.

Discipline Brings Freedom

Whether we accomplish it early or late in life, eventually we all must learn to discipline ourselves and our desires. Many lives have been ruined by uncontrolled appetites, which often run rampant in summer, with its relaxed and laid-back pace. There seems to be an increased desire then for more thrills, more indulgence, more possession of material things.

The irony to discipline is that it often carries a negative connotation. We believe disciplining ourselves is done at the expense of limiting our freedom. We think that more of one means less of the other. If we step back for an objective view, it becomes obvious that freedom and discipline are not trade-offs. There can, in fact, be high freedom coupled with a great amount of discipline. Freedom occurs when we voluntarily impose self-discipline, when we set our own goals, when we impose order on ourselves.

Self-discipline is essential for self-renewal, and summer is a good time to renew ourselves mentally, emotionally, spiritually. Most of us go through life only partially aware of our abilities, because getting to know ourselves is the most difficult thing we can do—and the most inconvenient too. We always employ an enormous variety of clever devices for running away from ourselves. In his book *Self-Renewal*, John Gardner once said, "More often than not we don't want to know ourselves, don't want to depend on ourselves, don't want to live with ourselves. By middle life most of us are accomplished fugitives from ourselves."

Without discipline, there is no order in our lives. The most self-reliant, self-governing man or woman is always under discipline, and the more perfect the discipline, the higher will be his or her moral condition. So, before another summer comes to a close, hopefully we will take some time for personal reflection and realize that self-mastery—the ability to govern ourselves properly through self-discipline—is the only road to true and lasting freedom.

Goals Bring Growth

Thoreau reminded us that "men were born to succeed, not to fail," but the line between success and failure may be so fine that we scarcely know when we pass it. Often, we throw up our hands at a time when a little more effort, a little more patience, would have achieved success. Persistence can turn what seems to be hopeless failure into joyous success.

There is no failure except in no longer trying. Failure is not in falling down, but in staying down. If there is a single factor that makes for successful living, it is the ability to draw dividends from defeat. We are more likely to conquer difficulties when we believe in our own ability to do so. And this confidence in ourselves can inspire the confidence of others. It is a contagious kind of courage that carries others along with it.

A young man with great potential—stricken in his prime with a crippling disease—inspires all those who know him. Despite his affliction, he always finds the strength to maintain an attitude of optimism. He reads, he writes, he studies. He finds courage and comfort in the scriptures. He sets goals for himself. He became engaged and he married. And although travel is both difficult and painful for him, he and his bride left by car on their honeymoon. Upon returning, he wrote in his personal journal, "Next time we plan to travel south. After that, who knows? I hear Hawaii makes a great winter getaway."

Courage, faith, optimism. Yes, Epictetus told us that "difficulties are the things that show what men are." It is always possible to better our lives—to seek values and opportunity in any situation. Attitudes, said a prominent psychiatrist, are more important than facts. A handicap is a fact. Hardship and disaster are facts. But where one person is defeated by a handicap, another is stimulated. Where one merely complains about hardship, another rises to the challenge. Poet Joaquin Miller, inspired by the log of Columbus's first voyage across the uncharted Atlantic, wrote, "What shall we do when hope is gone? . . . Sail on! sail on! sail on! and on!" Men were indeed born to succeed, and to succeed at overcoming difficulty is the greatest success of all.

A Success Secret

There's an old Babylonian proverb that says, "If a man be lucky, . . . [you can] pitch him into the Euphrates and like as not he will swim out with a pearl in his hand." Some modern writers have also suggested that there are those who continually stumble into prosperity, in spite of themselves. And so it seems that some people have all the luck. Success follows them as surely as noon follows morning. They are the ones who rise through the ranks of any group to emerge as the leader, who have full checking accounts, whose dreams don't turn to dust in their hands. Or so it seems.

Too often our attempt to be like one of them, to move into a more satisfying life, is actually no attempt at all. We wait, thinking some lucky break will come our way and change our life. We think something will arrive in the mail or someone will notice our hidden talent, and then we'll move ahead. Or we wait for tomorrow, believing it will feel different than today—and when it comes and it doesn't, we wait another day.

But the truly successful have a different approach—quite the opposite from waiting. It is action. When an opportunity comes their way, they grasp it. If they have a good idea, they believe in it and won't shake loose. An eminent medical pioneer is said to have a sign on his desk that reads, "I've been lucky. The harder I work, the luckier I get."

In sum, what the truly successful seem to do is to crush the spirit of procrastination that haunts them as it does every human being. They have learned that a hesitant heart will lead them nowhere. They have discovered that the security that comes from never risking failure is no security at all. Earth, after all, is not a safe place to be, and the safety-seeker who procrastinates his best intentions and his best dreams for fear of failure must soon realize that he is not safe anyway. Life is a daring adventure or it is nothing.

We must trample the voice that suggests to us that tomorrow would really be a better day to try. We must crush the whispers that say, "You can't," and ignore those who say, "You're not capable." Those who seem lucky are really those who put aside their fears and doubts and, with the secret knowledge of their own inadequacies, gather together the determination to start today to be what they really want to be.

Defeating Discouragement

A characteristic aspect of people who succeed is an unwilling-ness to admit defeat. Many a cause has been won long after the cause seemed hopeless simply because there was a soul who refused to be discouraged, who saw beyond the specter of defeat the bright hope of success and believed in it.

Of course, failure and defeat are a part of life. The only persons who have never failed are those who have never tried; the only ones who have not tasted the bitter legacy of failure are the ones who have not risked devotion to a cause. They who would succeed must understand defeat and not be defeated by it. And it is possible to know defeat and not be defeated. Because in the words of the hymn, "There Is a Balm in Gilead," there is a moment of succeeding and hope beyond all our momentary failures and despair.

Too often we are impressed by the limitations of our lives; too often we focus on failed dreams and unfulfilled expectations; too often we see not the seacoast—the vast and hopeful bounty of the sea—but sand that winnows through our fingers and cannot be held. Certainly, there are those who have talents and abilities greater than our own; there are those who perhaps have suffered less, who have gained more. But God does not measure us one against another; he does not value our lives in the context of others' living. As the hymn promises and persuades us:

> *If you cannot sing like angels,*
> *If you cannot preach like Paul*
> *You can tell the love of Jesus,*
> *And say "He died for All."*

God did not make us to be defeated. Indeed, he sent his Son as a sacrifice so that ultimately we might succeed. That ultimate success does not mean there will not be moments of failing. But we are inspired by the Light of Christ to take hope in our succeeding, to not be too quick to have failure define our experience, and to realize that failure does not in itself predicate defeat. We are defeated only if we are stopped, only if we linger in failure and do not see beyond it to the hope of other opportunities. We are defeated only if we fail to see a brighter, more significant eternal success that ultimately will diminish every failure and save every soul who finds it out.

ADVERSITY

Peace, Be Still

Threatening clouds hung dark overhead. Angry waves crashed against the small boat in which the disciples of Jesus huddled helplessly before the howling wind and rolling waters. Jesus slept calmly in the back of the ship. Finally his terror-stricken disciples awakened him and begged him to save them. Jesus stood and commanded the stormy sea and sky with these words, "Peace, be still," and it was calm. The disciples turned to one another and said, "What manner of man is this, that even the wind and the sea obey him?" (Mark 4:38-41.)

Jesus' words were a command to the elements, but they might also be taken as counsel to his disciples, and to us. Clouds of war and nuclear holocaust hang over our world. Violence and crime threaten us. Corruption and immorality weaken the supporting structure of this ship we call civilization. In laboring to keep the ship afloat we may find our backs aching as we bend to the oar, our hands calloused and bleeding, our faces stung by the driven spray. At times, we may feel we are fighting the elements alone. The Lord, for our own good and for his own purposes, may choose to not take a direct hand in the struggle. It may sometimes seem to us as it did to the apostles that the Lord is asleep and has left us to save the ship alone.

But such is not the case. When we are doing our best to carry on righteous works and still appear to be sinking, we may call with confidence, "Save us, Lord, we perish." And that which we ask he may well give. He will sustain us and bless our efforts. If the occasion demands, he will rebuke and command the very elements that his work may not be swamped and submerged in the depths of sin and evil. He has done so in the past. He can do so in the future.

There will be injuries, even casualties, in this contest of good and evil. And there is no promise that the ship will sail smoothly; but sail it will. And those who hold to the course the Lord has marked out will find that they make steady progress even in heavy seas. And amidst the roaring waves they may have an inner peace and quiet comfort in knowing the Lord is with them. In these troublous times what greater blessing could a loving Father in heaven offer his children than the assurance that he is watching over them. Blessed are all those who accept his promise and enjoy his peace.

Facing Problems

Every year in much of the northern hemisphere we enter the long, gray season when life seems a little harder for want of sunshine. We battle flu bugs and stalled cars, try to buoy sagging spirits against long, cold nights, and through it all wonder why life has to have so many frustrations. We think that tomorrow or next month or even next year will bring us ease. Surely at some point the obstacles will fall, the little problems that bite at us like a swarm of angry insects will subside. That is the time for which we yearn.

In reality, though, those who are the sturdiest and happiest among us have learned a secret about problems—a secret, perhaps, that is the source of the happiness that lights their way. It is this—that there is no tomorrow or next month or next year when life is suddenly easy. Ease was not promised us as one of the conditions of mortality. If we are to be happy, it must be despite the fact that life presents challenges—not by fooling ourselves that someday they will go away.

The happy among us know that life is essentially a problem-solving experience. They expect that life will hold its anxieties and are not baffled when it does. The issue is not whether we will

36

have problems, but how we solve them or react to them. Many are angry when a problem arises, consider it a great injustice, a wart upon the face of experience. We sometimes ignore our problems, hoping they will go away. We pelt at them with our fists in rage, or we devise wonderful escapes. But these devices eventually fail.

If we would be happy, then we must finally admit that life will present us problems in one form or another nearly every day. Once we admit that, we are made free of that sense of injustice that usually accompanies a problem. We won't continue to ask, "Why me? Why today?" We'll take problems as a condition of life and gear ourselves to face them and fight them. Wrote one poet, "Let nothing ever grieve thee, distressed by life's problems." Said a successful businessman who conquered obstacles along the way: "If there is a problem, there is a way to solve that problem." When we admit problems are part of the fabric of experience, we can face them; and when we face them, we can find power to solve them.

Never Give Up

Several years ago a young athlete crouched poised in the starting blocks at the beginning of the high hurdles competition. Behind him was a good part of his lifetime spent in dreaming, training, working, planning and building for this moment. Ahead of him was a chance for the highest of all trophies, an Olympic gold medal. At the gun he shot out of the blocks and streaked down the track. But he misjudged a hurdle, fell, and in a fraction of a second the dream of a lifetime slipped out of his grasp.

He was asked many times the obvious question, "Was it worth it?" Always his answer was the same, "Yes. It isn't how many times you fall in this life that counts, it's how many times you get up." Thus it is with each of us. None of us is so talented and skilled that we will accomplish all our dreams without skinned knees, bumped noses, or occasionally falling flat on our faces. If we go through this life with no failures, it will mean simply that we set our goals too low.

One of history's great examples of tenacity and perseverance is Winston Churchill. When England was on her knees, and most of the free world was reeling from the blows of the Nazi war machine, Churchill hurled his famous challenge to Hitler. Tough as an old English bulldog, he stood before the House of Commons and thundered, "We shall never surrender." And they never did.

The same principle holds true whether we are defending a nation or building a life. It is the making, not the having; it is the trip and not the destination; it is the next pinnacle beyond the one on which we stand that gives life its zest and gives promise to tomorrow. And the greatest of all the gifts of God to us is the promise that those tomorrows can go on forever; that growth and continual climbing can be ours, and with them the ever-enlarging vistas and the joy that comes with accomplishment. So when life is difficult and dreams are far distant, be assured that if they are good and worthy, they will come to pass even if it takes some portion of eternity.

After the Death of a Loved One

It seems incomprehensible to those who mourn the death of a loved one that the world keeps turning, that shops are open for business as usual, that newspapers and bills are still delivered, that neighbors and friends continue on their casual way. This is especially true for those who lose a partner in marriage, a companion through long decades of growing and changing. When death takes a spouse, much of our own life also dies, leaving us withered and unwilling to continue. Even with the healing hands of time, some are never able to fully overcome the traumatic and awesome effect of their spouse's passing. Theirs, unfortunately, is a world of pulled window shades and mementos from the past, a world where the present and the future are nonexistent.

But there are others who with time rise from the ashes of this human tragedy to become even better and stronger, not in forgetfulness of the past, but in appreciation for the future, in gratitude for each new day of life that provides another opportunity to experience, to enjoy, to serve.

These are some examples: One widow from a small Western town began sharing her gift for candy making with friends and relatives. Now whenever the need for encouragement or cheer arises, her delicate candies, symbols of her own kind nature and disposition, are sure to appear. A retired math teacher who lost his wife some time ago now spends much of his time as a volunteer in an alternative high school. It is a rough neighborhood; the students in the program are outcasts and dropouts. But where others have failed, he is succeeding. And in so doing he is enriching the lives of his students as well as his own. And finally, a widow of only short duration now enters the doors of a local hospital almost daily to assist wherever help is needed, with paperwork, with the small chores of medical care, or with a more important task for which she is eminently qualified: to sit, quietly, lovingly, with those who wait as she once waited.

The list is endless; countless men and women have risen from despair and bewilderment to bless the lives of others. Theirs is the knowledge that human life consists of human service, and that a meaningful life and service to others are one and the same.

The Usefulness of Sadness

Sadness and melancholy are feelings we would generally avoid if we could, but of course we cannot. Joy and sorrow are mixed and stirred together to make up the substance of our lives. The Roman poet Ovid knew that fact when he wrote, "No pleasure is unalloyed: some trouble ever intrudes upon our happiness." And modern psychology seems to confirm this viewpoint. Dr. Norman Bradburn wrote, "Happiness is resultant of the relative strengths of positive and negative feelings rather than an absolute amount of one or the other."

Happiness seems universally accepted as a desirable state in our lives, but what is the purpose of sadness? The somewhat pessimistic preacher of Ecclesiastes had high praise for sorrow when he wrote, "Sorrow is better than laughter: for by the sadness of the countenance the heart is made better." (Eccl. 7:3.) It could be debated whether sorrow is better than laughter, but most certainly it has an ofttimes unappreciated value in our lives. We can learn lessons in moments of melancholy that would escape us if all our days were filled with sun and smiles—lessons of patience, endurance, long-suffering, and courage in the face of adversity. And these lessons we might well ponder in our pleasure-seeking world.

We are daily indoctrinated to believe that sadness is unnatural, that life should be one steady stream of joy and laughter, and that if we are not happy there is something wrong with us. This shallow view of life can lead us to unfortunate conclusions. Young married people may seek divorce at the first signs of difficulties, not knowing that every marriage has its problems. Others of us may go deep into debt to try to buy our way out of depression.

As a people we have grown so intent on living lives free from all sorrow that we now seek stimulants and tranquilizers, drugs and panaceas at the slightest sign of sadness. While sometimes medication may be necessary to get us through a crisis, we should not let it rob us of the healing and the strength that we can gain in facing our afflictions and working out our problems. A bit of melancholy contemplation can be for the injured heart and mind what rest and recuperation are to the body, a chance to let life's inner powers work and mend and heal the injury, the trauma to the soul that brought about the sorrow. Yes, sadness is a part of life, and while we do not seek for sorrow, neither do we fearfully flee from it. Oftentimes the shadows gathering about us allow us to more clearly discern the light of the Lord's Spirit as he sends it forth to lift us and guide us on our way.

The Role of Suffering

Of all man's questions regarding human existence, the problem of suffering seems to be one of the most perplexing. For some individuals, pain and suffering appear to be punishment from God for sins committed or laws broken. Others see it as an indication that there is no God: for surely, reason these people, an omnipotent God could have organized a universe without the presence of pain and sorrow. And for others, the question remains an unanswered riddle.

No single conclusion completely answers this question concerning the role of suffering. In one sense, it is punishment brought on by our own doing, for much pain and suffering is the consequence of man's own actions. Unwise decisions, greed, envy, and other forms of ignorance have their own natural results. And just as the child is burned from touching the hot stove, so, too, unhappiness is the predictable outcome of breaking the eternal laws of heaven. These consequences, however, are not arbitrary punishments from a spiteful God, but natural results of disobedience to just laws.

But not all suffering is punishment. Indeed, it seems at times that the pure and innocent suffer the most in this existence. The newborn infant may be stricken with defects at birth; untimely death through accident or disease sometimes overtakes the loveliest and best of our friends; and Jesus himself, the most innocent of all, suffered in agony upon the cross at Calvary.

These facts, however, are not evidence that God is non-existent or that he is not powerful. Rather, they are evidence that he has used his wisdom for the benefit and education of mankind. "Sorrow is knowledge," observed Byron. And to this Henry Giles added, "The capacity of sorrow belongs to our grandeur; and the loftiest of our race are those who have had the profoundest griefs because they have had the profoundest sympathies."

Thus, the divine qualities of patience, charity, and empathy for the pains of others are many times born and nurtured through suffering. For God to withhold a knowledge of the world's pains and wrongs from his children would be to deprive us of our humanity, leaving us ignorant of the lessons of heaven. Even with this, our understanding of suffering is not complete. Faith is still required: faith that God is, faith that his divine administration extends to the human situation, and faith that his love is that of a kind and eternal parent.

Overcoming Problems

A problem, like a child's exercise in mathematics, seems something to be solved according to an easy formula, set aside, and then forgotten. Certainly that's what we hope for in life.

Sometimes under our breath, we pray, "Let it not be too hard today." We look forward to a time when the difficulties will level off. We think that after a challenge has passed, after a sickness is spent, or after the closets are organized, then will come a time of peace. Not so.

Problems are a condition of personal mortality, the ebb and sometimes inconvenient flow of a world where we are only visiting. There is no security from them. Helen Keller, who ought to know, is quoted as saying this about security: "It is mostly a superstition. Security does not exist in nature, nor do the children of men as a whole experience it. Avoiding danger is no safer in the long run than outright exposure. Life is either a daring adventure or nothing."

But sometimes the danger of living can almost overwhelm us. We wonder if we can manage our problems or if they will manage us. We could handle them if they would come one at a time with sufficient breaks, but too often they flood us. We frantically search our resources and seem to come up empty.

That is when we need to remember the great message of the gospel. To God nothing is impossible and we are not alone. We were not born to fail. He who has known us longer than we can remember can give us back to ourselves. However much evidence we may muster to the contrary, he knows that we have the power within us to meet any problem with his help. Eleanor Roosevelt reportedly used to carry the following prayer in her purse: "Our Father, who has set restlessness in our hearts and made us all seekers after that which we can never fully find, keep us at tasks too hard for us, that we may be driven to Thee for strength." We must never doubt that he can deliver.

The Uses of Adversity

"Sweet are the uses of adversity," wrote Shakespeare. That is counsel we might well keep in mind. The adversity and sorrow we go through may be bitter, but the experience may leave us wiser and more compassionate human beings.

The greatest lessons of this life are gained from experience.

The finest doctors are not those who have only studied medicine but those who also understand suffering. The staunchest fighters for freedom are those who have been in bondage. The most dedicated teachers are those who have felt the stifling handicap of ignorance. And the wisest spiritual counselors are those who have seen the sad effects of sin. We are in this world to learn and grow through experience, and sometimes that growth is painful. Even Jesus Christ we are told, "learned . . . obedience by the things which he suffered." (Heb. 5:8.)

Likewise each of us will experience some grief and sorrow in this world. The richest, most powerful, most intelligent, most resourceful of us cannot escape what Hamlet called "the slings and arrows of outrageous fortune." Physical disease, accidents, the inevitability of age, darkness and depression, sorrows of the spirit and emotions, troubles and tragedies—any or all of these can strike us. Ultimately there is no insulation against the stresses, strains, and sadness of this life.

These trials can be to us a crushing burden; or they can be a refining fire to purge from us the trivial cares and concerns that can cloud our vision of what is really important in our lives. This kind of learning will not come easily, but the truly valuable things in life never do. The adversity will not be sweet, but the uses and results may be if we triumph over our tribulations.

May we remember this when sorrow strikes us in large or small measure. Remember that God is still in his heaven. There can be a purpose in our pain, because some of our most priceless wisdom comes only through experience. And if we endure it well, eventually our grief will be turned to gladness.

The Strength from Adversity

Life is so basically good, and we so expect it to be good that occasionally we become frustrated and confused by the adversities that may appear to stand in the way of our happiness. There may even be those who ask, "If God loves us, why does he not protect us? Why does he not keep trouble from afflicting us?"

The most immediate answer to that question is that he does.

He does love us, and frequently he answers our prayers with deliverance. Are not the scriptures filled with songs of gratitude such as the one found in Psalm 30:1-2: "I will extol thee, O Lord; for thou hast lifted me up. . . . O Lord my God, I cried unto thee, and thou has healed me."

But sometimes, too, God may appear not to intercede. Sometimes we are blessed not with miraculous deliverance, but with the lesson of adversity. The eighteenth-century British statesman and orator Edmund Burke taught that "adversity is a severe instructor, set over us by one who knows us better than we do ourselves, as he loves us better too." Indeed, from adversity, from challenge, from difficult moments and potentially defeating circumstances have come some of mankind's noblest moments.

Seventeen years ago the American educator and concert pianist Leon Fleischer was stricken with an undiagnosed case of carpal tunnel syndrome. The result was that he lost control of the fingers of his right hand. He could no longer play the piano—a potentially devastating tragedy for a man who had been a child prodigy, who had dedicated much of his life to performing on the concert stage. But the artist devoted himself to his teaching; he began conducting; he did not utterly despair. In 1981 an operation restored the use of his right hand. Subsequently, he returned to the concert stage. But of those intervening years when his dreams seemed ruined, he says, "There is no doubt that what seemed like the end of the world to me in my little life turned into an opportunity for growth, for expansion and a widening of horizons."

So it often is with adversity. We must pray for God's help in our lives; and he will help us. Sometimes the adversity that is best put aside will be put aside. And for that adversity that does not leave, he will make us strong enough to bear, and the stronger for having borne.

FAITH

By Faith All Things Are Possible

Faith is the key that unlocks the door of success for every human being. We all exercise faith at various times in our lives. It comes in all degrees and in all quantities. The scriptures tell us, "Whatsoever thing ye shall ask in faith, believing that ye shall receive in the name of Christ, ye shall receive it." (Enos 1:15.) Faith can heal the sick, bring comfort to those who mourn, strengthen our resolve against temptation, help us overcome harmful habits, and give us the strength to change our lives. Faith is the source of New Year's resolutions . . . and the power that makes them work.

It takes faith to develop a strong personal value system, to stand up for what we believe, to lead a disciplined life, to control our appetites and our yearning for material things. It takes faith to make the Sabbath more than just another day of the week. It takes faith to make prayer a daily habit. It takes faith to keep God's commandments. If we had greater faith in ourselves and the truth of God's help—which he freely offers each of us—we could accomplish many things. It is a power by which all things are possible . . . a power we all have but only the wisest among us use consciously.

Of course, there must be a beginning point—a place to start building faith. We are told in Romans 10:17 that faith comes by hearing the word of God. Throughout biblical history we read of those who developed strong faith. It was by faith that Moses led Israel through the Red Sea, that Daniel stopped the mouths of lions, that Peter and Paul raised the dead. By faith Noah prepared an ark for his family. It was faith that sustained Abraham when asked to place his son, Isaac, upon the sacrificial altar. (See Heb. 11.)

The Lord has challenged us: "Prove me . . . if I will not open you the windows of heaven, and pour you out a blessing, that there shall not be room enough to receive it." (Mal. 3:10.) Unfortunately, many people never accept that challenge. They don't fulfill their human promise and potential because they lack the necessary faith to change their lives, to set new goals and to experience personal growth. Faith makes it possible to know that, even in temporary failure or setback, there is always a next time—always tomorrow. It provides a sense of direction that is sorely needed as we move one year closer to the twenty-first century. Every one of us can develop a more positive outlook on life. We can achieve, conquer, overcome—all by anchoring our lives on the rock of faith.

Faith Makes a Difference

The Savior said: "Suffer little children, and forbid them not, to come unto me: for of such is the kingdom of heaven." (Matt. 19:14.) Many scholars believe this statement refers to the *faith* of children, who truly believe in "the substance of things hoped for, the evidence of things not seen." (Heb. 11:1.)

We begin life with an unquestioning faith. As we grow older, that faith is tested by the experiences and events of life. Often, our faithline hits bottom during the years of early adulthood. At that time we make one of life's most important decisions: will we allow our faith to continue its decline, or will we take steps to begin rebuilding faith?

Usually, the decline of faith is gradual. It is influenced by the weight of responsibilities that bear on us as we approach adulthood, as we come face to face with the demands of life. We become aware of the weaknesses and strengths of those around us. We have experiences which challenge our faith. But if we are fortunate and wise, we learn that faith does make a difference in life. We learn that faith in a Supreme Being is the single most powerful force we can use to overcome our problems, to understand our situation, and to make life meaningful. Faith is most important where knowledge is imperfect.

We cannot have perfect knowledge about the many demands of living. We can believe that God exists, and that the life he created has purpose beyond our understanding. That kind of faith gives us reason for living. It grounds our existence. It gives solidity to our lives. It helps us venture boldly into the unknown. But as the decline of faith was gradual, so too must the rebuilding of faith be a gradual process; and, most of all, with commitment—commitment expressed in the love of God and the understanding of his divine purpose.

Each of us can remember the unquestioning faith we had as little children. Our goal as adults is to re-create and re-direct that faith, for as the Savior said: "Whosoever shall not receive the kingdom of God as a little child, he shall not enter therein." (Mark 10:15.)

Faith in God

The Lord encourages us to have faith: "Come unto me, all ye that labour and are heavy laden, and I will give you rest. Take my yoke upon you, and learn of me; . . . and ye shall find rest unto your souls. For my yoke is easy, and my burden is light." (Matt. 11:28-30.) Faith in a supreme being is the single most powerful force we can use to overcome our problems. It helps us endure extraordinary hardships without losing our perspective. With faith we are never alone.

As we begin to understand the process of faith, we realize that we can change our circumstances by changing our attitude and exercising faith. It is true: we are literally what we think; our character is the complete sum of all our thoughts. God will always base our individual trials of faith on our particular temperaments and dispositions. The thing that will test one person's faith will not necessarily test another's. But when we humble ourselves,

49

fully realizing that we cannot succeed without the Lord's help, he will extend himself to us.

The Lord wants us to have faith in him. And if faith is difficult, he suggests that we experiment and exercise a particle of faith. If that is still difficult, he tells us to simply have a desire to believe, and he will enlarge our souls and enlighten our understanding. (See Alma 32:27-28.) In the words of the hymn by Franz Schubert, "The Lord is my shepherd; I shall not want. . . . He leadeth me beside the still waters. . . . He giveth peace unto my soul."

Faith

We often discuss the role of faith in the affairs of men and women. "Faith is the substance of things hoped for, the evidence of things not seen." (Heb. 11:1.) It necessarily permeates every aspect of our lives. For instance, the state of world affairs—with wars and rumors of war—can be disheartening. But we overcome our despair by having faith in our country, faith in its leaders, faith that nations can resolve their differences and move in the direction of peace. And we learn from experience that whenever illness or adversity strikes, the best prescription is faith.

When businessmen share their formulas for success, they call it positive thinking, but it is really nothing more than faith and the will to succeed. Faith often marks the line between success and failure—a line so thin we scarcely know when we pass it. All of us have had the experience of giving up too soon, of throwing up our hands at a time when a little more effort, a little more patience, and a little more faith would have achieved success.

A great deal of the unhappiness and vice in the world is the result of weakness and indecision—products of failing faith and collapsing courage. Those who are undisciplined, who have no faith or inner strength, are severely buffeted by every temptation that comes along. For these individuals, life is often difficult and unhappy.

But of all the creatures on earth, man alone can change his thought patterns and become the architect of his destiny. If we understand the process of faith, we can change our circumstances by changing our attitudes and exercising that faith. Those who think about faith as a principle of power realize that there is virtually no limit to what they can accomplish. Faith—or lack of it—can determine how we feel, think, and act. It can determine our values, what is important in our lives, and how we cope with problems. It can give direction, purpose, and meaning to daily living.

Faith takes many forms—from belief in our friends, to belief in a better tomorrow, to belief in God. Of all the expressions of faith, that which should have the highest priority is religious faith—faith in the Savior, faith in his teachings and commandments, faith in his prescription for living a rich, full, and rewarding life. This need for religious faith and the peace it brings is well expressed in the lyrics of the hymn, "Jesus my Savior true . . . Teach me a better life. . . . Be thou my beacon light; Guide me to thee."

The Enemy Is Fear

Here in the United States, we have grown increasingly concerned about the health of our economic system. Indeed, the eroding effects of inflation seem to be eating away at the values of currencies in almost all nations. In this country, the value of the dollar has decreased rapidly during the past decade, while the incomes of many individuals have risen slowly.

The consequences of this economic sickness affect almost everyone: the young couple's dream of owning their own home must now be postponed, at least for the time being; providing for the educational and temporal needs of children is becoming increasingly difficult for parents; and the retirement hopes of older couples are being frustrated as savings are used up to pay the demands of present-day living.

As with malignant diseases that attack the human body, the causes of this economic tumor are complex. No doubt, deficit spending by governments and by individuals is partly to blame. Recent declines in the rate of worker production along with the great number of individuals in our society who consume without producing must also bear some of the responsibility for these inflationary times. These contributing factors must be dealt with in the same way the causes of any disease are handled: they must be isolated and eliminated as much as possible.

There is, however, one other factor that is more injurious to our economic system than these, and even more harmful than the inflation itself. That factor is fear: the fear that the future will not alter the maladies of the present, the fear that the economic structure will collapse altogether, the fear that the traditional values that have made in our nation a strong and vibrant economic system are no longer relevant. Fear itself is the greatest threat to our economic survival.

The antidote for fear is faith—not an ill-founded faith that believes that everything will resolve itself without work or sacrifice, but a confidence that has been personified by tens of thousands of businessmen in this country, individuals who have proven that the tenets of free enterprise are sound, individuals who have placed their talents and resources on the open marketplace and have reaped the dividends. It is this faith in hard work, honest production, and open competition that will provide the remedy for our present ills.

May we overcome our doubts. May we accept the gift from him who conquered all fears and said to us: "Peace I leave with you, my peace I give unto you. . . . Let not your heart be troubled, neither let it be afraid." (John 14:27.)

Science and Faith

From the beginning of time, man has debated the issue of faith versus science—which is right. Upon close examination, the premise that science and faith are incompatible does not hold true.

In the first place, it is faith alone that gives validity to the conclusions of science. No scientific discovery, large or small, has ever been made without the exercise of faith. The astronomer, scanning the heavens for cosmic truth, relies on faith as the basis for his observations: faith that the senses accurately transmit truth, faith in the reliability of his machinery, and faith in the observations of others that add to his own knowledge. Alike, the philosopher searching for reality with his math and logic must trust in the rational faculties of man as a primary premise to his determinations. In reality, science without faith is lifeless.

Nor does faith exist independently of science. Whatever the object of our faith, its source participates in the scientific process. The man whose faith in God is strengthened through an observation of the inherent design of nature is using the same senses for his conclusion concerning God that the astronomer uses for his conclusions concerning the cosmos. And even divine inspiration speaks to the soul with the same call for logic that science employs. "Come now, and let us reason together," said the Lord to Isaiah. (Isa. 1:18.)

Thus, science and faith are not combatants, but comrades in search of the same truths. It is only shallow science that fears faith, and shallow faith that fears science. And so we would remind those whose faith excludes science that faith in God is not the enemy to experience, reason, or even doubt. And we would suggest to those who discount faith—because it is not a perfect knowledge of things, but a hope in things unseen—that science itself is not certain; for during man's long search for truth, much of what was once called scientific fact is now called old superstition. There are and will be truths that science cannot know, truths pointed to by the spires of our chapels and temples, truths attainable only by the infinite reach of man's faith.

PRAYER

The Sweetness of Supplication

There is a great deal of satisfaction to be had from independence, and we all seek to be self-sustaining: to use our God-given talents for the purpose of earning our way in the world. But in our efforts to become independent, we must remind ourselves that we depend upon what we are given as much as upon what we earn. Life itself is a gift, and the sweetness of a gift is not that it is deserved, but that it is joyfully given and gratefully received.

Children seem implicitly to understand the importance of receiving and of asking. That may be one of the reasons why Jesus said, "Suffer the little children to come unto me, and forbid them not: for of such is the kingdom of God." (Mark 10:14.) Children understand their dependence, and they teach us by their innocence. The joy children take in living teaches us the importance of life; the energy and enthusiasm with which a child lives teaches us how to grow; the openness and the unashamed asking of a child teaches us how dependent life is upon him who gave it. When children innocently request their hearts' desire, believing that they may receive, we learn the sweetness of supplication.

Prayer is important not simply because it satisfies our needs—because we receive what we ask for—but because it develops and maintains a communion between Father and child; it teaches us our true relationship to our heavenly parent. We depend upon our God. And whatever independence we achieve is in direct proportion to our recognizing that dependence and to our supplicating God in prayer. Sweet is the hour of prayer when it springs from the soul of a loving child, a child who may be gray with years, but who recognizes that true independence is the gift of God, and that only through a supplication for God's guidance can true independence be achieved.

Our First Need

We do need the Lord every hour, but one of our challenges is to know in what way. One of the basic principles of economics is that needs and wants are unlimited, but resources to supply those needs are not. So goods and services must be shared and apportioned out in one way or another. The system of the Lord, however, works on different principles. The resources of heaven are beyond the measure of man, and the Lord is a generous provider. He is ever solicitous of our welfare, anxious to help us. He stands at the door and waits for our knock. He promised "[I will] . . . open you the windows of heaven, and pour you out a blessing, that there shall not be room enough to receive it." (Mal. 3:10.)

Why then, with such a vast celestial storehouse to draw from, do so many of us go without the things we need? There are no doubt a number of reasons, but one of the problems lies in not knowing what to ask for. There is a grain of truth in the wit of Oscar Wilde. He said, "When the Gods wish to punish us they answer our prayers." Many of the things we pray for would be a curse instead of a blessing if the Lord gave us our way, sometimes even when we ask with the best intentions.

Some years ago a forest ranger was stranded in a blizzard with his team and wagon. Back at his cabin his wife and children prayed fervently for the freezing temperatures to rise so their father could make it home, but the thermometer plummeted even lower. They had almost given up hope when they heard outside the bells of the horses and saw their husband and father approaching. The bitter cold had frozen the snow so solidly that he was able to drive home on the crust of it. If the Lord had answered this woman's prayers and warmed the weather, her husband would have bogged down in the snowdrifts and died from exposure.

How many of our needs are like that? We may think we need more money, but what we really need is the self-discipline that can come with more modest means. We may feel we need more attention and concern from others when what we really need is the chance to serve and take our minds off ourselves. There are times when we think we need rest and relaxation, but in reality we would feel better by increasing our effort. We may think we need power and prestige when we really need humility. On the other hand, the humble young man Saul had to be dragged from hiding at his own coronation. He needed to become a king.

Our first need then is to know what our needs really are; and how shall we know except we prayerfully consider, weigh the alternatives, establish our goals, and look to where we would like to be. Then humbly let us ask the Lord for confirmation that these truly are our needs. We may be confident that, as we make ourselves ready, our needs will be met in the Lord's time and in the Lord's way.

The Patience of Prayer

We live in an impatient world, a world in which the speed of our arrival seems to be valued even more highly than the importance of our destination. Fiber optics, bubble memory, communication satellites—even our communion with one another insist on speed. We telephone across the ocean nearly as easily as across town; we retrieve in milliseconds seemingly limitless information from our computers.

And yet, there are communications that defy our need for speed, messages that cannot be instantly commanded: the love that a parent gives a child, which takes years to develop and a lifetime to prove; the gestures of friendship that cannot be spoken in a moment, cannot be communicated in a word.

And prayer: In Jeremiah 29:12-13 the Lord says: "Then shall ye call upon me, and ye shall go and pray unto me, and I will hearken unto you. And ye shall seek me, and find me, when ye shall search for me with all your heart." We cannot express our "hearts" in a moment, nor quickly make them prayerful. Like the other communications of love and need, prayer requires persistence and consistence, a constant, willing turning of our souls to God.

Not that God needs to be reminded by our repetitions, but we do. We need quite literally to insist on his love—like the importunate widow of Christ's parable, who won her case before even an unworthy judge. We need to insist the merciful caring of the great judge of all. Because only if we insist, to ourselves as much as to him, only if we persist, will we develop that relationship of love upon which the communication of prayer depends.

God will respond, but his response depends upon our ability to receive. For that reason, the impatience that a busy, hurried world inspires works against the inspirations of prayer. If we are to seek God, and find him, we must find time for prayer, and the patience for our prayers to be answered.

Prayer Power

During a winter month in one of this country's northern states, an eleven-year-old boy was playing with his friends when a wall of wet snow collapsed on him and buried him alive. Helplessly pinned with his arms behind him, he felt the snow stiffen and freeze, entombing him and paralyzing his body. Soon he would die of suffocation. Meanwhile rescuers frantically dug through the snowslide as rapidly as they dared and pushed long poles into the snow to find him. Nothing worked until one of the rescuers turned to a powerful force. Moments later the young man was found, and his life was saved. The power that saved him was prayer. The rescuer who found him offered a prayer for guidance, and it was answered.

Yes, the power of prayer can literally guide us and save us, and it can bring us other benefits as well. As Fyodor Dostoyevski wrote in *The Brothers Karamazov*, "Every time you pray, if your prayer is sincere, there will be new feeling and new meaning in it, which will give you fresh courage, and you will understand that prayer is an education." Guidance, courage, comfort, education—these and other blessings come from prayer. It's unfortunate that we don't draw on this power more effectively to bless our own lives and the lives of those about us.

Perhaps we feel that prayer is mysterious, beyond our comprehension. And yet we casually put a plug into a wall and immediately tap power that may have been generated hundreds of miles from our home—power that was stored in coal or oil or gas, the power of a billion raindrops falling on a distant mountain, coursing in a river, and being captured by a hydroelectric generator. We may even be drawing power from the submicroscopic world of the atoms as they whirl and smash in their unseen orbits. Mysterious? Incomprehensible? For most of us, yes. But how dark, cold, and inconvenient our world would be if we refused to use electricity because we did not understand everything about it.

And thus it is with prayer. We may not know quite how it works, but we don't need to. The Lord has not burdened us with complicated formulas. He has made the process of prayer so simple that a humble child on his knees can make it work. The only requirements are that our desires be righteous and our supplication be sincere. The Lord stands ever anxious to assist us. "Ask, and it shall be given you," he said. (Matt. 7:7.) Many marvelous things are done every day in our world of wonders, but it may be that when the histories of mankind are compiled, we will find that the world was preserved not so much by the works we did each day, as by the prayers we offered each night.

The Gift of Prayer

Prayer has been a recurring theme on this program. We've commented about the continual need for prayer, about the strength and confidence it brings into our lives. We know that prayer is used not only in healing the sick, but also in maintaining good health. When patients under stress begin to practice regular prayer, their blood pressure drops, digestion improves, tensions dissolve.

I suppose we sometimes wonder if God actually answers our prayers. Students in a religion class recently discussed the subject. Their conclusion was that God hears all our prayers, even though he may not always respond the way we want him to or expect him to. It has been suggested that God may feel real anguish himself because he desperately wants to help us with all of our difficulties but realizes the need for us to have growth experiences that come through adversity.

But there is power and comfort in prayer, even if we do not receive the answers we seek. It allows us to verbalize our concerns. Prayer is an intimate conversation with a close friend. In times of stress we often think: "Oh, if only I had someone to talk to." Our Father in heaven can be that someone. He does listen, and he does care. And the opportunity to articulate our problems is in itself a psychological release. In that sense, at least, prayer is always answered. But sometimes we don't listen to the more direct answers that come to us. As one religious leader observed, the answers to prayer come quietly. They come when we are relaxed and not under the pressure of appointments.

Perhaps we do not hear at times because we tend to complicate our lives in this fast-moving world. How often do we allow a few moments for quiet meditation after we pray instead of rushing back into our daily activities. Imagine what we might hear . . . or feel in those few moments . . . or how our lives might change . . . or the lives of others. Prayer is a great communication tool, a divine gift given to each of us. It is real. It will work. Yes, the Lord will communicate with each of us if we will but give him the opportunity.

The Words of Prayer

Prayer is man's way of communicating with the Lord. He has instructed us in its use, even given us examples to follow. And through experience we have learned that there are many forms of prayer. But the most common—and perhaps the most difficult—is to pray with words.

Why words—those often clumsy sounds that seem to cloud as much as they communicate? "Words (are) but winds," said Samuel Butler. Why should we need to speak words to the Lord? He's ever mindful of us. He knows our needs better than we know ourselves. Perhaps it's because we, not God, need the words. The discipline of trying to put feelings and ideas into words can focus our attention and our thoughts. Whispering quiet thanks unto the Lord can have a humbling effect upon our souls. Enumerating blessings can bring gratitude, and speaking our requests can help us separate our idle wants from real needs.

Our words in prayer should be the best we have to offer. But whatever they are, if they are our best, is good enough. The lisping murmur of a child's first prayer finds equal welcome in the heavens with the poet's polished supplication. Of course, smooth flowing phrases from the lips and not the heart are not a prayer. Vain repetitions were condemned by Jesus, and certainly his model prayer does not contain a wasted word. The phrases are as clear and simple as a child's recitation, but their depth has never yet been plumbed by the most profound philosopher. In sixty-six words the Lord's prayer speaks praises unto God and links up earth and heaven. It speaks of earthly things like daily bread, temptations, and our tendency to hold grudges against each other. It closes with a promise that the woe and wickedness that typify this world will one day pass away and heaven take their place.

As it was to those who listened centuries ago, so should it be to us a worthy pattern for our prayers. For there is in all the sacred writings no more beautiful example of how words can take our thoughts to heaven than the Lord's prayer.

LOVE

The Tie That Binds

As we look at society we see not merely individuals, but groups—couples, families, towns, cities, governments. Wherever we find a society, we find people bound together by caring, sacrifice, and hope. It is this ritual of love by which societies survive. There may be sociologists who will argue for more complex motives of mutual need, of social Darwinism, but mere survival cannot ultimately explain our devotion, our cleaving to one another as families—families in which sacrifice, not survival, is the defining element of our love.

Recently in a remote area of southern Utah, an elderly couple was caught in a late-winter snowstorm. Their car went off the road, and they were stranded many miles from the nearest town. After waiting for a time in the refuge of their car, the couple decided to walk on to the next town or farmhouse. They walked all night, the eighty-five-year-old man leading his eighty-two-year-old wife through the snow that had begun to drift over the road. And in the morning all they could see were miles of mountains and rolling, empty hills.

For three nights they slept in the melting snow. For three days they scouted the muddy countryside, searching for help and helping one another. And on the morning of the fourth day, the old man died. His wife now remembers the moment when she realized he was not merely sleeping: "The dying took ten years off his face," she says, "and as much as I wanted and needed to be with him, I wouldn't have wished him back. What I wanted more than anything," she says, "was to lie down beside him and just let the world go."

But she didn't. It would have been the easy thing to do, but instead she survived several days longer until rescued by a search party. She survived the cold, survived the amputation of her left leg and right foot; survived even that amputation more painful to her—separation from the husband she had lived with and loved for more than half a century.

Why? She gives a single reason: "One of us," she now says, "had to live to tell our children, and our grandchildren, and our great grandchildren; one of us had to live to tell them what happened." Here is a story of survival. But not "survival of the fittest"—survival because of sacrifice. She survived not out of any personal desire, but out of love—a love for others, a love to give. It is that tie of love that sustains us, that rescues us from solitude. It is that tie of love that binds us to one another and brings us home to tell the story of our sacrifice, and our love.

Love One Another

The most basic commandment in Christianity is that we love one another. Jesus said on this and on our love for God hang all the law and the prophets. But if love is such a desired virtue, why is it so difficult to attain? Part of the difficulty may lie in our definition of love.

No word in our language has been so misused and abused. It is used in the most exalted forms of adoration, awe, and respect to describe the love of God. But then we speak of love in rather everyday experiences such as loving ice cream or chocolate cake. The word *love* is even twisted and deformed to describe the most sordid kinds of lustful desires. Surely these experiences and others we categorize under love are not the same emotion.

What then is love? No definition can be all inclusive, but a closer analysis might clarify what we mean. The ancient Greek philosophers described three kinds of love. They spoke of *eros*, which they defined as romantic love. Romantic love at its best is a beautiful thing, but the Greeks recognized that this was not the only kind of love in the world.

They spoke also of *philios,* or brotherly love. This is the love that inspires fraternities, social gatherings, ethnic and national pride. Brotherly love does much good in the world. It can warm our hearts and make us feel secure among our friends. But this form of love likewise has limitations. It is usually restricted to those who are similar to us, and it excludes those who are different. They are out of the brotherhood.

There is a love that transcends these limitations. The Greeks named it *agape.* Agape asks nothing in return for the love it gives. It does not require that the recipient of love be beautiful, desirable, or even friendly. Agape is for enemies as well as friends. This kind of love does not come easily. It may take a lifetime to achieve. It is the most unselfish of virtues. And though not easy, it is possible, and the rewards that come from practicing this principle are worth any effort to attain it.

As with other forms of love, the definition is in the doing. The Savior knew this, and so he made his life an example that we might follow. He loved his enemies, did good to those who hated him, and prayed for those who persecuted him. And he left us the commandment, "Love one another; as I have loved you." (John 13:34.) Agape—an unselfish Christlike care, concern, and love for each other is the only way we will ever find peace: peace in our own hearts, peace among neighbors, and peace for this war-weary world.

To Love

Speak to one another of love. We all have feelings of love, of being loved, of being in love. Why is it that this means so much to us? It is because love is the essence of the human experience. Oh yes, love is fickle and some think love is blind. But we will do for love what we would never consider for any other purpose.

We define the depth and quality of a person's love by that person's willingness to sacrifice. We would not take seriously the love of someone who said, "I will love you, so long as it does not cost me anything, so long as I need not change to love you, so long as my love is economical."

One of the evidences of love is the ability to sacrifice self.

69

Sacrifice is the evidence and virtue of love. Without this sort of "sacrificial love," there would be less silliness, fewer sentimental poems, perhaps even greater reasonableness in the world. On the other hand, there would also be no heroism, no charity, no feeling. And so, in spite of the burden that it sometimes is, in spite of the fretting bother that it can bring to our lives, we know that love is essential, fundamental to humanity. And the inability to love, freedom from the need to be loved, is neither independence nor clarity of vision; it is an emotional deformity.

"Walk in love," Paul told the Saints of Ephesus, "as Christ also hath loved us." (Eph. 5:2.) And to the Saints of Thessalonica he said, "The Lord make you to increase and abound in love one toward another, and toward all men: . . . to the end he may stablish your hearts unblameable before God." (Thes. 3:12-13.)

And what of love of God? We learn to love God through loving mothers, fathers, sons, daughters, husbands, wives, neighbors. Indeed, true love does not obscure vision; true love is the one means by which we can truly see. Scottish poet Robert Burns wrote a poem of love, "Flow Gently, Sweet Afton," a poem that speaks of quiet, heartfelt expression; a poem that reminds us in a moment of tenderness that to love and be loved is to see more clearly than is possible in any other way.

Love Is a Verb

Among the parts of speech common to the English language is the verb. As we learned in early grammar, the verb is an action word, a word used to express motion or exertion. When we classify any word as a verb, we mean that it symbolizes an act, a deed, something accomplished, something done.

The word *love*, among other things, is a verb. Indeed, as it is used in the New Testament by Christ, the Author of love, it is almost always associated with specific actions or deeds. To love our neighbor, as Jesus described it, is to feed the hungry, clothe the naked, visit the sick. To love our enemy is to pray for him and treat him with kindness, and even to turn the other cheek. And to love God is to keep his commandments.

In each case, love is defined in terms of action. Christian

love, then, is not only a principle, a thought, or an expression. To be properly defined it must go beyond theory to active demonstration and application. The first and great commandment to "love the Lord thy God with all thy heart, and with all thy soul, and with all thy mind" and the second commandment to "love thy neighbour as thyself" (Matt. 22:36-39) are therefore a mandate to act. It is no more possible to truly love God and man without action than it is to transmit light by memorizing Einstein's theory of relativity.

The divine love of God toward his children is also based upon the principle of action. Because of love the universe was organized, the stars and planets set in their respective orbits; and man, the spiritual offspring of God, started upon the path to eternal life. It was the sublime love of Christ that led him to the cross to act out in agony his final demonstration of universal affection. Thus it is that all of our own charitable feelings and intentions toward humankind weigh less than one single act of love. The thoughts and words of love require works of love. For *love* is a verb.

When Love Transforms Duty

We do many things in life out of duty. We pay our taxes, follow speed limits when we're late, come back to work after lunch—all in the line of duty. And many of us classify obeying God as a similar action. It is duty. We worry that he is peeking around some corner waiting to pounce on us if we disobey. So with faces tight as army sheets, we grimly do what we think is right, reading the scriptures when we ache to read the paper, gritting our teeth and paying donations, checking off our list of Christian attributes with fixed determination.

Now, duty has its place, of course. We admire it for what it is. It is a marvelous schoolmaster, a bell that stirs us from our slumber, a stick that reminds us that life is larger than our own small passions. Like children who would rather play in the sunshine than learn arithmetic, we sometimes, perhaps often, need duty to motivate us into higher action.

But let us never be blinded into thinking that duty alone is enough to transform our hearts and take us back to God. It is far too weak a current. At some mysterious point, love must transform duty as the morning light transforms a pool of ice. We must obey the Lord not because we fear him, not even because it seems the right and proper thing to do. We must obey him finally because we love him. We ache to serve. We yearn to be like him who is the center of our highest ideals and our fondest affection.

It is no accident that the Lord said, "Blessed are they which do hunger and thirst after righteousness." (Matt. 5:6.) Hunger and thirst are words we understand. They tell us something powerful about our human needs. As Kakuzo Okakura said, "Nothing is real to us but hunger." Love is another word with that kind of passion that cracks through barriers of the heart and moves us when nothing else can.

Yes, the Lord will take our actions born of duty and even bless us for them, but let us understand that there is more. It is love that writes a symphony, a fine novel. It is love that leads a parent to a child's bedside. And finally, it is love, and only love, that can lead us back to the Lord.

The Lifting Power of Love

One of the greatest messages the Savior taught and exemplified was love. Not only did he love us enough to die for us, but he taught that we should love one another. What power there is in that admonishment.

What power there is in love. Love poured out upon a wasted, wilted life can make it bloom as beautifully as water does the thirsty flowers of the desert. People privileged to develop in a climate of love become securely rooted in a sense of their own worth and abilities. Love begets in us an honest acceptance of ourselves and our fellow human beings. We begin to see beyond our faults and frailties to the potential perfection that is in each of us. Carl Sandburg wrote:

> I love you for what you are, but I love you yet more for what
> you are going to be.
> I love you not so much for your realities as for your ideals. . . .

72

*Not always shall you be what you are now. You are going
forward toward something great. I am on the way with
you and therefore I love you.*

We are all going forward toward something great. We need
not fear the forces that would try to hold us back, whether they be
forces from without or from within our own timid souls. "There is
no fear in love," said the apostle John, "but perfect love casteth
out fear." (1 Jn. 4:18.) We need to trust the gentle pulling power
of love that draws us upward toward the Lord. And we need to
show our gratitude to him by stretching out our hands in love to
lift the lives of others. We need to love our neighbor and ourselves
and God. . . . For only as we love all three can we become what
we can be.

Loving God

Seeing what love God has bestowed on us, his children,
should create in us a sense of obligation, a duty to return in kind
the divine and personal affection we receive from our Father in
heaven. Indeed, the first and great commandment is "Thou shalt
love the Lord thy God with all thy heart, and with all thy soul,
and with all thy mind." (Matt. 22:37.) As the supreme commandment, this principle reveals the most important aspect of the
gospel of Jesus Christ, the central theme of all that has been
written in the law and spoken by the prophets.

Well, loving God sounds like an easy task. To love a being
whose only concern is for our temporal and spiritual welfare
should not be too difficult. But perhaps there are a couple of
reasons why loving God is not as easy as it sounds. First, if we love
God, we will keep his commandments. And second, we cannot
love God without also loving our fellowman.

Love is a verb of action. We cannot demonstrate affection to
Deity with pure adoration alone. No, if we love, we must also act.
To love God, then, is to love the truth that is found in his
precepts and commandments. In this sense, love and obedience
are synonymous. If we love God, it follows as heat follows fire that
we must keep his commandments.

It is also impossible to love God without loving all of humanity. For that reason the second commandment, that we should love our neighbor, is similar to the first, that we should love God. The two are coexistent. To endeavor to love God while despising the man next door, or on the next street, or in a foreign country, would be the same as an attempt to utilize the solar energy contained in moonlight; the process would yield very little light and no heat at all. So too the love we send to God must be as pure and direct as sunlight; it must not be contaminated or diluted by hate and prejudice.

And finally we should suggest that loving God is not only a commandment but also a natural response to that tender care we receive from a devoted father; it is a response that can only take the form of our obedience to his commandments and of our unconditional love for his children.

On True Love

One of the problems with verbal language is its inability to adequately express abstract thoughts or feelings. Take, for instance, the oft-spoken phrase, "I love you." Three syllables, three short sounds, uttered daily wherever English is spoken; and yet this simple phrase can represent a wide variety of feelings or thoughts. When whispered between the young couple, across a candle-lit table or under a full moon, "I love you" suggests romance, desire, or idolization. But when exchanged between those who have weathered long seasons of marriage together—periods of financial distress, the responsibilities of parenthood, sickness, and even tragedy—the words "I love you" may have quite a different meaning.

It is to this notion of mature love, which many times begins as infatuation, that we turn our thoughts today. The enduring nature of true love sets it apart from its fleeting counterfeit. That is not properly called love which dissolves when confronted by adversity or change. Indeed, genuine affection cannot be altered by the transitory factors of circumstance because it has nothing to do with extrinsic things. It is, rather, an attachment to the intrinsic qualities of character, qualities that do not alter with changes in appearance or possessions.

Love is not love that wavers with the turns of fashion; nor does it falter with time's theft of youthful looks; nor will it disappear with the failure of health or prosperity. It is as Shakespeare wrote: "An ever fixed mark that looks on tempests, and is never shaken." No, true love is not a weed that sprouts overnight, spontaneously along the roadside, without forethought or care. Authentic love is a more exotic plant. It is a hybrid flower that must be nurtured and developed through the entire season of marriage; a flower that must be cultivated in a soil rich in respect and mutual understanding; a flower that blossoms only in a climate of patience, consistency, and continuous kindness. As the Scottish poet Robert Burns observed about true love, "My Luve's like a red, red rose . . . and I will luve thee still . . . till a' the seas gang dry, . . . and the rocks melt wi' the sun."

MARRIAGE
AND
FAMILY LIFE

Successful Marriage

Despite rumors to the contrary, there has been an upsurge in recent years. More and more couples—both young and old—are entering matrimony. And an increasing number of these weddings are being performed by the clergy. These are good signs of a healthy society; they are encouraging, hopeful signs in the face of many signals that would have us think marriage is becoming unpopular. Hopefully it never will.

Marriage is perhaps the most vital of all decisions we make in life. It has the most far-reaching impact. And happiness and success in marriage is not just something that happens. A good marriage must be created. It requires constant, continuous nurturing. The little things are the big things—caring, courting, giving, and forgiving. Each partner must be as interested in the other as in himself or herself. That is the only basis on which love and marriage can be successful.

All too often marriages fail because partners focus on what's wrong with their lives rather than what's right with them. Couples must build upon the positives. If the talk is negative and full of problems, it creates a negative outlook. Conversely, when a couple constantly exchanges words of love and support, it creates an atmosphere that in itself will help to sustain and build their happiness. Couples should safeguard each other's self-esteem, developing a mind-set where each is tuned in to the other's positive qualities. In a growing relationship there is no room for constant criticism, sarcasm, nagging, and fault-finding.

A successful marriage brings many benefits. Couples are physically and emotionally healthier. And stability at home overcomes many of the uncertainties in life. In a twenty-four-year study recently completed, satisfied couples identified companionship as their greatest satisfaction. The signs are encouraging, and our continuing interest in marriage is easy to explain. Marriage is the cornerstone of a strong family, and the family is the foundation of society. Wherever the family flourishes in a state of vigor and unity, there will also be found a strong and sound society.

A False Escape

Marriage is perhaps the most vital of all the decisions we make in life. It is a union of minds as well as hearts, with far-reaching impact. Yet for many, happiness in marriage is fragile and fleeting. Divorce provides a quick and slick escape route and for many has become a way of life. It seems no one is immune. And what is worse, it seems divorce is contagious.

A good marriage is built upon a foundation of compatibility, but the building material is adaptability. The causes of unhappy marriage and divorce often can be boiled down to one word—selfishness. If each partner is in marriage only for his or her own benefit, it is bound to fail. If both are concerned about the happiness of the other, it is bound to succeed. But it does take a commitment from both.

Divorce is usually a cop-out, a false escape. It begs the question of personal responsibility. It encourages the individuals to take the same problems to a new setting. Two law partners, with thirty years of combined experience specializing in marital problems and divorce, are convinced that, on the whole, divorce is a mistake—that divorce is wrong in ninety percent of the cases they've seen. The exceptions—the ten percent—involved cases of extreme cruelty, alcoholism, and perverse behavior. But they are a tiny minority.

Determination, loyalty, and commitment are the "glue" that holds couples together when they've lost their direction. With that "glue" and the Lord's help, marriages do succeed. "Thou shalt love thy wife with all thy heart," commanded the Lord, "and shalt cleave unto her and none else." (D&C 42:22.) The apostle Paul said, "Husbands, love your wives, even as Christ also loved the church, and gave himself for it." (Eph. 5:25.) "And unto the married I command, . . . Let not the wife depart from her husband: . . . and let not the husband put away his wife." (1 Cor. 7:10-11.)

Marriage is a series of compromises. We have to give and take, refrain and restrain, endure and be patient. We must focus on what's right with our lives, not what's wrong. We must build on the positive, not the negative. And marriage can be continually strengthened with words of love and support. Marriage *is* the most vital of all decisions we make in life. That is as it should be, because it is ordained of God.

A Happy and Good Marriage

Marriages would be more successful if each would try to make his partner happy rather than good. Making our spouses good, though, is a great temptation. We don't live with anyone very long before we see their faults. We trip over their inefficiencies and sloppiness, suffer for their moments of selfishness. We're stung by outbursts of anger and by things they've left undone. It doesn't take a genius to see how they could improve our lives—if *they* would only change. So, we make our lists, create improvement programs, and remind our partners frequently of their faults. Others may nag, but *we* gently suggest, and see ourselves as virtuous all the while. After all, our efforts are only for their good.

Well, there is nothing that does less good in marriage than vowing to change the other. Marriage ought to be a sanctuary from a painful world, a place to soothe our feelings and gain the strength to run another day. But it can't be if one partner is trying to remake the other. Then, instead, there is a discomfort, a feeling that home is a briar patch full of thorns where one does not quite measure up. Worse, the improvement programs we design for someone else rarely work. Growth is self-initiated. It is an inner striving to be more. We can't make someone kind or thoughtful. Fat people don't lose weight because someone else tells them to. We can no more mold someone than tell a flower when to bloom.

We ought to give up the futile idea of making our partners good and concentrate on making them happy. That starts by accepting our helpmate, faults and all, with unconditional love. It means noticing the thousand good things our loved one does every day and offering praise for them. No one lives with a perfect person. So let us not be surprised that we don't. For every change we'd make in our partners, they could list a change they'd make in us. So when we feel the urge to make somebody good, we can start with ourselves. When we want to make somebody happy, we can look to our partners. Ironically, if we make them happy, we'll go a long way toward making them good.

The Nineteenth-Century Home

Something has changed during the past century, something more than technology and life-styles, something more than our mode of transportation and our living habits, something we didn't see, and perhaps didn't want. It is hinted at in our houses, apartments, and condominiums—of which the majority are now empty for almost the entire day; it is suggested by the absence of leisurely family meals, which were once an everyday event; it is implied by our mobility, our constant moving from house to house; and it is intimated by an entire population of runaways, children fleeing intolerable conditions of abuse or neglect. This something, this change, is a profound shift in our concept of home. It is a change so dramatic and far-reaching as to threaten the very foundations of our social and political way of life.

The typical home of the nineteenth century was far different than most of the houses of today. It even appeared more secure and friendly: squarish homes of red or painted brick, heavily trimmed with wood, with porches at front and back, and picket fences between the lawns and the brick sidewalks that led to a sturdy protecting door. There were aromas too. In the morning there was hot oatmeal and breakfast biscuits. At noon, when children of the nineteenth century ran home to eat, there were the smells of baking bread and homemade soup; at evening, lasting smells of gravy and turnips, of meat and pudding. And noises have changed too. Then there were sounds of the piano from the parlor and the children from the kitchen, of mother placing the hand-dried dishes back in the china closet, and the final nighttime sound, heard from beneath the covers in the darkness, of father bolting the doors to hold us safe from the world and keep us protected by the encircling structure of home.

It was almost a living organism, the home of the nineteenth century. It had a quality that is largely lost today, a rhythm, a quiet routine, almost a dullness. But it was this syncopation of life in an ordered environment that bequeathed to its children confidence in self, trust in society, and faith in a friendly universe. Let us hope that the home of the nineteenth century is not extinct. Perhaps the kitchen smells and picket fences are gone forever. But these were only evidences of higher, more lasting laws—of strong family ties and belonging, of order and of parental contact—and with these, we can still make a house into a home.

Building Strong Families

The holiday season is an excellent time to enjoy our families. Those who nurture strong family roots watch their efforts bear fruit year-round. But the harvest is at its peak during the season beginning with Thanksgiving and extending through Christmas and New Year's Day. That is a time when families gather.

As we observe around us the many families gathering, some seem to be closer, more cooperative, and happier than others. They seem to be doing something right—and they are. Researchers have identified five common characteristics of strong families:

First, family members express appreciation for one another and make each other feel good about themselves.

Second, families with strong roots spend time together. They structure their lives so they can enjoy each other at meals, in recreation, and at work.

Third, strong families spend time communicating with one

another. They share their feelings openly, but they also listen well when others in the family are talking.

Fourth, family members are deeply committed to promoting one another's happiness and welfare. When life gets too busy or too hectic, they stop to reorder their priorities, making sure the family is at the top of the list.

Fifth, religion continues to be related to marital happiness and successful family relationships. And it's more than simply attending church together: strong families share a spiritual lifestyle. An awareness of a higher power helps them be more patient, more forgiving, quicker to get over anger.

The strength and character of the family has been a recurrent theme throughout history. Strong families have provided the foundation for every strong society. But the formation of strong families is not automatic. It requires the efforts of every family member. And families will only be as strong and as important as we make them.

The holiday season is a time to renew our commitments to building a strong family. It's a time to visit relatives and reinforce family ties. It's a time to make family life a top priority—not only for this season, but for the coming years as well.

Families Need Priority

Personal worth can be measured by the happiness one generates in the lives of others; and the lives over which we have the most influence are those of our own family members. No joy can equal the joy that comes from being part of a successful family, from building strong relationships, and from developing a feeling of togetherness, a feeling that family members belong to each other.

No family is perfect, but some parents and children seem closer, more cooperative, and happier than others. When the family has high priority, there seems to be a deeper sense of warmth and good feeling among family members, a harmony and oneness of purpose. There is a firm assurance that what individual members do and who they are really matter.

One of the common complaints in busy families when parents must juggle busy schedules is that there just isn't enough time. The characteristics of these overcommitted families include a continual sense of urgency and haste, a constant feeling of frustration about not getting things done, and a gnawing desire to find a simpler life. Many families experience these feelings at one time or another, but a relentless hectic pace means it's time for a reevaluation of priorities. Such a pace signals a need to seek more satisfaction from within the family rather than from outside activities.

In order for the family to remain strong, parents must realize that a family must be created, that family units must be built, that a good marriage and responsible parenthood must be worked at. Families require time and attention. Some individuals put personal gratification above the human and spiritual needs of their families, but the happiness these people thought would come to them through worldly ambitions always seems to elude them.

The great need today is for a strong sense of family, the need to slow down and enjoy one another, the need for love at home—love between husband and wife and between parents and children. A breakdown of love at home will bring a collapse of the family itself; and when the family goes, so does the nation. When we generate happiness in our homes, we increase not only the strength of the nation but our own sense of personal worth.

Strong Families Are Vital

Each day, we realize more and more the absolutely essential nature of the family. It is the foundation of nations, and despite rumors to the contrary, surveys indicate the family is stronger than ever. Although individual families are being challenged—and many face stressful situations—society clearly places top priority on the family as an institution.

Research reveals five main characteristics of a strong family unit: first, a sense of appreciation among family members about what they do for one another; second, a genuine enjoyment in doing things together; third, good communication among family members, including the ability to deal openly and constructively with conflict when it occurs; fourth, a commitment to each other and to the family unit, where the happiness and welfare of each family member is valued by the others; fifth, a high degree of religious orientation and participation in religious activities as expressed in a set of shared values and spiritual concerns.

Religious activity forms a strong foundation for family strength, and the most effective way to teach religion in the home is not by preaching, but by example. If we would like our children to have faith in God, then we must show faith in him ourselves. If we want to teach the principle of prayer, then we ourselves must pray. If we want our children to have self-control and live virtuous lives, then we must provide examples for them to follow.

A close family built upon a religious foundation promotes self-esteem among its members. Self-esteem is a key factor in learning, loving, and maturing. It is the key to a healthy mental attitude. A strong family promotes self-esteem in the only way self-esteem can be created—over a lifetime, a little bit each day. There are no instant miracles in building strong, mature individuals and citizens.

That is why the nation and the world need strong, stable homes—homes filled with love and understanding and support and unqualified acceptance. No nation can endure without good citizenship, and that kind of citizenship comes only from strong family units.

The Importance of Family

At a recent conference on families, speakers appealed for an America where the home is a place of love and stability . . . a place where experiences, dreams, joys, and sorrows are shared . . . a place where families are built on love that can span the barrier of generations. According to a Gallup poll commissioned for the conference, Americans clearly give the family top priority. Eight of ten persons ranked family life among the most important elements in their lives. Another public opinion poll indicated that Americans are more concerned about moral decay and its threat to the family than about inflation and economic conditions.

These are reassuring reports. They put the importance of the family back in perspective. We've heard and read so much about attacks on the family, about the breakup of families, and about the so-called alternatives to the family that it sometimes appears the family is losing favor in our nation. Apparently it is not. Americans continue to support the family as the basic unit of society. Stable families create a stable nation, because they are the most effective place to learn essential human values. The family is the most effective place to experience love. Love between husband and wife, love among parents and children, love that extends beyond the family unit to encompass neighbors and friends. And the family is the most effective place to teach love of country, love of life itself and of the promise of life.

The family is a strong social unit that must withstand pressure from without as well as turmoil from within. It is the foundation of society, the wellspring of the nation. As one educator, Neal A. Maxwell, said, "If we poison the headwaters of humanity—the home—it is exceedingly difficult to depollute downstream." We are encouraged—encouraged because the American people continue to place the highest value on the family, because they recognize it as the single most important unit in society.

The American Family—
An Endangered Species

During recent decades, our society has become increasingly sensitive to the various forms of life with whom we share the earth. Laws have been enacted to protect the habitats of numerous types of animal life. Endangered species lists have been established. On them are recorded the names of those animals that face certain extinction unless they are afforded protection and special consideration.

Well, there is another name that should be added to the endangered species list. It is a species whose survival at this time is in serious doubt, a species whose extinction would be tragic and irreplaceable. However, this species is not biological but sociological in nature. This endangered species is the American family.

The existence of the family as a close-knit group of individuals consisting of two parents and their children, working together toward common objectives, is threatened. The following statistics are evidence that the American family is in trouble: The divorce rate in America has reached the fifty percent mark—one of every two marriages now ends in divorce. The number of one-parent families has increased more rapidly in recent years than the number of two-parent families. There is an increasing number of children being born without the advantages of married parents. In 1940, one child in thirty was born out of wedlock; now the figure is one in eight. The average American father spends seven minutes a day with his children. American husbands and wives spend an average of twenty-eight minutes a week talking to each other.

This is only a partial list of indications that the basic unit of society is in danger. Conceivably, it is already too late to save this most valuable of all sociological species. Perhaps the family will succumb to the mounting pressures that threaten its survival and become only a chapter in future history books.

Hopefully not. We like to think it won't happen, and hopefully we'll be proven right. For the strength of the family is the strength of society. The survival of the family is linked directly to the survival of the community and the nation. For our own sake, and for that of our children, may we protect, maintain, and restore this endangered species—the American family.

PARENTHOOD

Train Up a Child

Centuries ago, King Solomon offered some parental advice to his people. It seems equally applicable today: "Train up a child in the way he should go: and when he is old, he will not depart from it." (Prov. 22:6.) No church, no educational institution, no peer group can have as powerful an effect on a child as do one's parents. The challenge is, as parents, how do we train our children, and what shall we teach them? Teaching the right things is not always easy, but teaching the wrong things can be. A wise teacher once said, "Ninety-five percent of learning is in modeling the behavior of the teacher." Certainly that is true with parents and children. Our examples are far more powerful than any platitudes we may preach to our children. Of course, we'll make mistakes, but we must strive for consistency. If we tell them to be honest and then lie to our neighbor, which lesson will be learned?

Children need to know when they are wrong. How else can they learn? People do not resent correction if done with love and kindness. Pearl S. Buck wrote, "Some are kissing mothers and some are scolding mothers, but it is love just the same, and most mothers kiss and scold together." The loving touch of a mother's hand, the gentle counsel of a father's voice, the security of knowing of a parent's love—these things teach a child the most important lessons of life: lessons of love, of personal worth, of consideration and compassion for others, of reverence for the Lord.

The home is where these values, standards, and beliefs are

learned. They are passed down from father and mother to child, but it is wishful thinking to assume our children will absorb these values spontaneously. They might learn from example to embrace the wrong standards, but they, like generations before and yet to come, will need direction and encouragement to find the proper paths for their feet. And then they will watch to see if what we say is consistent with what we do.

No matter how much information we accumulate in textbooks, or how elaborate our educational programs, there will never be a substitute for children learning at their parent's knee. Discussing ideas at the dinner table, reading together on the living room floor, strolling through a park discussing God's handiwork, or kneeling by a child's bed for evening prayer—these are the most priceless teaching moments in the life of any parent or child. In these simple settings, life's most important lessons are learned.

Where Father Lives

A father died and left a grieving child. "Where is my father now?" she asked, then paused. Scanning a family portrait, she saw his mark on every child, gene deep. One with father's dark eyes, another with his height, large hands on still another to cup with comfort a slumping shoulder. "That's where my father lives," she said. Then on into the day she went, and the clouds grew thick around her and the light fled until she knew fear. "The world is not a safe place," she said. "Where is my father now?" When others trembled and fell back, she kept walking, one footstep at a time, finding the only safety in her soul. "That's where my father lives," she said. She came upon an ailing friend along the road whom others hurried by. "When someone needs help is when they need it—not some other time," she had heard her father say. She had no time, but still she stopped. "That's where my father lives."

Every father leaves his mark upon his child more indelibly than in any other place. He may run a corporation, carve monuments to his greatness, create legislation in his name, but it is his child who will show the sure impression of what he was. "I want to be like my dad," writes the primary schooler, describing his ambitions—and he will be, too, socially handicapped or armed for triumph by the man who reared him. Consider the lessons of fathers.

A child's first sense of security may be because the father who knows the contradictions and injustices of the world protects him like the aspen does the seedling pine. The pine will know the weather soon enough. For now, it needs to establish solid roots. A child's sense of right may come because a father has uncompromising integrity. His actions are not based upon expediency, but values. Cheat a business colleague, go for greed, lie just this once when it's convenient? Never. A child's sense of compassion may grow because his father showed him that kindness is not weak. Stop for the stricken motorist, build another's confidence, help with the dishes? Of course. Jesus Christ told us that if we knew him, we would know the Father. We too are our father's child, and even when he's gone, some gesture, some holding on when it seems impossible, some rise of courage when all else fails us can let us know—that's where our father lives.

The Work of Fathers

Of what work may a man be most proud? Should he be proud to be a patriot? Should he be proud to preside over a great business corporation, command vast armies, occupy a seat of power in government, receive the cheers of thousands, be the subject of biographies? Such works should make a man feel proud indeed of his accomplishments.

But listen to the words of one man who lived just such a life and then looked back. "By profession," he wrote, "I am a soldier and take pride in that fact. But I am prouder—infinitely prouder—to be a father. . . . It is my hope that my son, when I am gone, will remember me not from the battle but in the home, repeating with him our simple daily prayer, 'Our Father Who Art in Heaven.'" General Douglas MacArthur wrote those words, and he was right. Our world needs good men for many things, but for nothing so much as to be righteous fathers. No number of brilliant statesmen, subtle philosophers, resourceful businessmen, or scientific geniuses can save us from chaos if we break the thread that binds our generation to the next.

We speak of the father of our country, or the father of modern science, or the father of endless other endeavors. But these are merely metaphors, shadows of the singular title a man assumes when he shares in the sacred act of creating another human being. Fatherhood is a responsibility that cannot be delegated or ignored. Every father will influence his child for good or bad. Traits of his mind and body will be part of the baby even before it is born. Virtually everything the father does will affect his child. No man can run so far or hide so well that his absence or presence, his indifference or concern, his cruelty or his kindness will not affect his child for good or ill. What a sobering responsibility and what an inspiring opportunity it is to be a father.

God bless the righteous fathers of this world. Men will do great works here on this earth for which they will be duly honored and duly proud, but they will do no greater work than bringing forth and "training up" another generation. (See Prov. 22:6.) It is significant that God, who could have chosen any awe-inspiring title in the universe, has asked that we call him Father.

Kiss It Better

A toddler awoke in the middle of the night crying for his mother and screaming in pain with an earache. She rushed to him, scooped him up into her arms, and then noticed that as he sat upon her lap, he pressed his ear to her lips again and again, seriously believing she could somehow kiss it better. Kiss it better. How many hundreds of scratches and bruises and cuts are presented to mothers each day with the plea, "Kiss it better." For to children, mothers seem to have some secret healing power, better than Band-Aids. It is the power of love.

And even when children have outgrown the idea that mother can kiss a hurt better, they still gravitate to wherever she is in the home. They bring their bruised and battered egos, shaken up from an indifferent world. They look to her to fortify them against fear and worry and self-doubt. They know she will notice when no one else does the little victory, the hidden beauty, for she has loved them longer than any other mortal person—loved them when they were yet a beginning, loved them when they looked at her out of eyes too new to focus, loved them when they stumbled over their own feet in learning how to walk, loved them when they faltered and failed in learning how to be.

While kisses may not heal cuts and earaches, unconditional love is full of healing. Mother's love is the most powerful force in the life of an unfolding personality. The mother's task is no small one. There are those who would diminish her power, equating motherhood with drudgery as if she scrubbed sinks and polished floors all day, instead of adding luster to eternal human beings. But really, her role in a smaller way is very much like the Lord's. His "work and [his] glory—to bring to pass the immortality and eternal life of man." (Moses 1:39.) Like that role, a mother's work is the main business of life, the development of personality. As the writer Anna Garlin Spencer noted, "Personality is above all the quality of unity, some individual wholeness that prevents the human creature from wholly losing himself in the whirl of things. To develop this, even in common measure in the average life, it seems to be necessary that at the point when the child is first making effort to become a person there shall be some quiet brooding, some leisurely companionship of the beloved, a rich and generous sharing of some larger life always near when needed" . . . a mother.

A mother is a healer in the truest sense of both physical and emotional hurts. She helps her child achieve wholeness through the power of her love—no small task in a world full of broken hearts and shattered personalities.

A Mother's Love

Political unrest, wars and rumors of wars, and the continuing upsurge in crime are indications that all is not well in human society. Turmoil and conflict seem to be the earmarks of our age. Much of the solution to these dilemmas, however, will not be found within the chambers of the world's parliaments, nor in the laboratories of science. Our hope for a more peaceful world lies at the spring of human affection and goodwill—a mother's heart.

It is there, surrounded by the warmth of a mother's love, that a child first finds a sense of belonging. A mother's presence is the first and most enduring evidence that there is love in the world. The impressions she implants influence the course of life through this existence and beyond. Thus, it is not necessary in order to honor mothers that we coin new phrases or express new thoughts. That which has been expressed in the past is sufficient. For the single unchanged truth in this modern world of motion and complexity is the ever constant and unconditional nature of a mother's love.

A mother is the one fountain of love that never diminishes or turns bitter. Regardless of our failures, in spite of our weaknesses and doubts, whatever the sin or indiscretion, no matter what others may think of us—a mother still loves on. There is no distance, in space or time, that can separate us from the lullabies and caresses of childhood. The baby is soon the adolescent, the adolescent soon the adult. Too soon the child is grown, and the playthings of youth are carefully put away. The girl of ringlets and giggles is now the wife, the mother; the boy of baseball and engines is now the husband, the father.

But to our mother, we will always be her children. Her hopes and fears for us remain; the pride at our accomplishments, the empathy with our defeats. Without condition, without compensation, her love endures, and will endure as long as days are without number, as long as she remains—a mother.

Just a Mother

What a mistake it is to think that motherhood is outdated or menial, or that being a mother is not prestigious. Common sense rejects this false notion; history contradicts it; and truth disproves it. And yet, how often we hear this apologetic response, "I am just a mother," as if the title needed defending.

Just a mother . . .

"My boy is not stupid," said one such mother when her son

brought home a note from a teacher saying the boy was too stupid to learn. "I will teach him myself." She produced Thomas Alva Edison. Just a mother brought refinement and culture into a nineteenth-century peasant cottage in Poland—Madame Curie, Nobel Prize winner and benefactor of mankind, was the result. "All that I am, or hope to be, I owe to my angel mother," concluded one man near the close of his life—a man who had spent his boyhood in a log cabin and had gone on to occupy this country's White House and to save a nation and emancipate a people: Abraham Lincoln.

Just a mother . . .

Men are what their mothers make them. Not governments, not schools, not churches—but mothers are the fundamental architects of great men and great women. To mothers alone is entrusted the awesome responsibility to train the mind of an Einstein, to light the poetic flame of a Longfellow, to instill the compassion of a Florence Nightingale, or to nurture the genius of Michelangelo. From wherever we stand, we look back toward the hazy dimness of our childhood whence we came and, with moist eyes, acknowledge the font of our learning and character—our mothers. Just a mother—acting confidently and responsibly in her role as human engineer, who is unfearful of ridicule, is unmindful of fame, and does what love bids—will cast the shadow of her influence over the world.

She Is His Mother

With memories of home and infancy, we turn again to thoughts of mother. We have learned the heavenly lesson that has waited patiently for us, biding its time, until we could understand that a mother's love is the most constant and the most unconditional human affection that this life has to offer. It is at once irrational and divine, defying the analysis of logic and science. It is the one gift among all God's rewards that is offered without condition or stipulation. It is a mother's love.

Picture, if you can, this scene: the medium security visiting room of a large American prison, with drab gray walls, folding

97

chairs, and silent, well-armed guards. There, too, wait the Sunday visitors—friends, wives, acquaintances—all waiting as they have waited many times before, as each prisoner is summoned from his cell to be properly accounted for, and brought in in turn for this brief meeting, this short-lived interlude between the endless moments we call a week.

Among these guests this day, these faithful guests, sits a graying woman—a large and wondrous woman, waiting patiently, calmly reserving one chair near her side. We see them enter one by one, this hapless file of hardened criminals, crafty counterfeiters, thieves and outcasts, some mere boys, while others show the lines of age. We watch with her as he appears. We note the flippant nature of his amble and surmise the scorn that lies not too distant from his lips. To us, his is a brutal, savage face. But to her, to her who brought the infant into being, who stood above the crib and proudly rocked the newborn boy, whose lullabies for him have never ceased though time and circumstances have argued for his guilt, to her the face is sweet and soft. Regardless of the crime or evidence, to her he will always have a form of innocence. There is no infamy or callous deed with which to alter her unchanging love. And even to the hour of her death his name will still be held in reverence.

For whatever else he is, he is her son. And she is his mother.

LIVING
THE
GOSPEL

Service to Others

When the judgment day arrives and our lives are reviewed, we will probably be judged in large measure by whether we were kind to other people, not by whether we accumulated wealth, social status, or material things. The judgment will be based on what was in our hearts and what we did for others.

The great principle taught by the Savior—whose birth we celebrate at the end of every year—was one of service and unselfish concern for our fellowman. The ability to be the servant and not the served requires a peace of mind, an understanding of that which is of greatest worth. It is an attitude that comes from within the soul. At any given time, we may lose our strength, our money, every single possession, but we will never lose the happiness in our lives if we serve our fellowman.

The Rev. Theodore Hesburgh of Notre Dame has suggested three qualities intimately associated with service to others: First, compassion—the human quality of sensitivity, the ability to suffer with those who suffer, to be moved, to reach out, to understand. Second, commitment—without which we are likely to live for ourselves alone (which would be a poor and valueless life indeed). Third, consecration—a quality with religious connotations. The qualities of compassion and commitment are difficult to achieve unless buttressed by religious motivation to help us overcome the urge for personal selfishness and self-centeredness. That's what the Lord is telling us when he says we have to lose our lives to find them.

The end of the year, presaging the start of a new year, is an excellent time to find ourselves in the brotherhood of man, to share our love, and to expound "peace on earth, good will to men."

Choosing Good

One of the most intriguing paradoxes of human nature is our capacity to encompass virtue and vice, strength and weakness, righteousness and sin in a single soul. Each of us is not merely strong or weak, but strong and weak, depending on the moment and the challenge. This is how we are, but not how we were designed to be. God did not intend us to be paradoxes to ourselves. We come into this world innocent, free of sin. But the influence of a fallen world corrupts us. And our insensitivity to the promptings of our Creator makes all of us, at one time or another, weak to temptation. Nevertheless, there are many people whom we judge to be virtuous; not because they are absolutely good, but because they have so magnified and encouraged the good in their lives that it overcomes temptation.

This choosing of good is what God intends: choosing the right way—not because we are unable to choose otherwise, but because we desire righteousness. So it is that the greatest challenge many of us will face is not in choosing between the good and evil of this world but in choosing between the strength and weakness in ourselves. This paradox of choice has been our chief challenge since the first man and woman left the Garden of Eden and faced a world that did not naturally support them, a world that was not inclined to encourage their righteousness.

God requires that we choose *for* the good that is in us and *against* the evil that is in the world in order to find a place in his kingdom. He is understanding of our failure and has provided the sacrifice of his son Jesus Christ that we may repent of our wrongdoing and choose once again the right way. He, who unlike us is eternally righteous, who does not change or waver, understands and forgives our wavering and encourages us to change from our sin. He calls to us that we might forsake our vacillating between the good in ourselves and the evil in the world, that we might put aside the paradox of our lives and become one with him as he is one with all that is virtuous, lovely, of good report and praiseworthy. If we will but choose him and his way—though we may be weak, though at times we may fail—yet through repentance and the power of divine sacrifice shall we find the good that is in God . . . and in ourselves.

The Eternal Value of Virtuous Living

Virtue is like beauty: it has intrinsic value. We need not be told that if we are good we will receive a reward; for the truly virtuous person, goodness is its own reward. But like our appreciation of beauty, our appreciation of virtue is mutable, and virtues have a way of coming in and going out of fashion. Where meekness once was valued, people now look for assertiveness; where simplicity of spirit once was sought, people now seek sophistication. Where once temperance was fashionable, people now are praised for their passion. In a world so changeable in the virtues it values, one might be led to wonder if there are any absolute values, any virtues that are more than conventions of social convenience.

To such a question we answer that the truly virtuous is like the truly beautiful: it is eternal. In the mind and eye of God, the beautiful and the good have always been, and they will always be. Only our imperfect perception leads us to believe that they change, that the virtues of yesterday are inappropriate for today.

Insofar as we seek to temper virtue to our need rather than to temper ourselves by its discipline, we are less adequate to achieve even those virtues we value. For instance, the virtue of passion— of loving, and believing, and sacrificing—has no enduring flame unless fanned by the discipline of temperance. The virtue of a sophisticated understanding is without value if not married to the simplicity of a virtuous life. The virtue of assertive leadership must be directed by the meekness a leader expresses in his willingness to be led.

A virtue, even when it is less fashionable, is of no less value in our lives, because virtue is not merely an adornment; but like beauty, it has value in itself. The reward of truth is honesty; the reward of love is loving; the reward of courage is a life not lived in fear. In each virtue we achieve there is an immediate, intrinsic reward in the sort of person we become, the sort of life we create. Such creation is beyond the mitigations of fashion. Because it, like the virtue from which it springs, is eternal.

The Fourth Commandment

One of the more interesting and important aspects of the Ten Commandments is that they are as valid today as they were when Moses came down from Mt. Sinai. We need to be reminded from time to time of their application today, of the need to still keep the Lord's commandments and observe his teachings. Perhaps one of the least observed commandments by today's generation is the fourth: "Remember the sabbath day, to keep it holy. Six days shalt thou labour, and do all thy work: but the seventh day is the sabbath of the Lord thy God." (Ex. 20:8-10.)

The commandment to keep the Sabbath day holy has never been rescinded. The Lord gave the day as a gift—a day of rest, a day for good deeds and kindness, a day to withdraw from the concerns of the workaday world, a day to enter into the fulfilling world of the spirit. It should be the best day of the week. But for too many, the Sabbath is just another day—another day of business or another day of play. Perhaps there is a connection here between that attitude and a recent national poll that suggests a lack of religious strength in America . . . a glaring lack of knowledge about the Ten Commandments and the basic tenets of our religious heritage.

Religion provides meaning and direction in life. But many people become so immersed in daily life that they ignore eternity. They look no further than their next paycheck or to the next weekend Sunday outing. Without a foundation of spiritual value, our lives become hollow, meaningless, and empty. The law of Christ is the law of inner perfection—of overcoming weaknesses, of motivating ourselves to higher performance and spiritual commitment. Such laws help us set proper goals and define our values. The Sabbath day is a day set aside to do that—a day to help us better understand our purpose on earth.

All faiths agree. We need a quiet time and place in which to see ourselves as part of the great pattern of things, to measure ourselves and our activities. It reminds us that we are not alone, that a higher intelligence has designed our course. As we communicate with the Lord, we receive the blessing of peace, and with it the renewal of strength. This peace and strength give our lives a truer perspective of what is and what is not important. The Sabbath provides an opportunity for inward searching and outward humbling of self. If we commit ourselves to keeping that day holy . . . to worshipping our Father in heaven, we will find our lives expanding and our happiness growing.

Giving of Ourselves

Albert Schweitzer once told a graduating class, "I do not know where all of you are going or what you will do, but let me tell you simply this; unless you set aside some portion of your lives to help and serve those less fortunate than yourselves, you will really not be happy." It is a point worth remembering. We may lose our strength, lose our money, lose every single thing we possess. But we will never lose the happiness in our lives if we continue to serve others. Many things are beyond our control. But service to others comes from within the mind, from within the soul. It is an attitude controlled internally by our own will or desire.

The Rev. Theodore Hesburgh also said to a graduating class that if he had his way, "Service to others less fortunate would be an expected and integral part of education for all Americans." He said service is part of the "dues" we should pay for our great good fortune as a nation. Service, said Father Hesburgh, may be "for all the generations to come, the only real way of keeping America great." The compassion and commitment required for service to others are often supported by religious motivation. We are told in the scriptures that when we are in the service of our fellowman, we are in the service of our God. (See Mosiah 2:17.) That is the great lesson of life we must learn, that our lives are not fulfilled if we do not give of ourselves. Such service should be given freely, without the desire for recognition.

Recall the story in the New Testament of the good Samaritan who gave of himself at great personal risk. Remember the teachings in the Sermon on the Mount, which are largely devoted to our relationships with other people. And don't forget the Golden Rule: "All things whatsoever ye would that men should do to you, do ye even so to them." (Matt. 7:12.) Yes, our relationships with other people in large measure determine not only our own happiness but also our standing before the Lord.

Guidelines for Life

When we think of the Savior's importance in our lives, we realize that his teachings are as relevant today as they were nearly 2,000 years ago. He asks us to keep his commandments—to be faithful but not fanatical. He wants us to be obedient, but more importantly he wants us to examine our motives. He tells us not to conduct ourselves merely for show and the praise of man. He warns us that the time of greatest success can be the time of greatest danger. He knows that pride is often a stumbling block in keeping the commandments. Ironically, when we are successful and things are going our way, we may be tempted to believe we've done it all ourselves.

C. S. Lewis observes in *Mere Christianity* that one of the dangers of having money is that we may be quite satisfied with the kinds of happiness money can give, and so we fail to realize our need for God. He says that "if everything seems to come simply by signing checks, we may forget we are at every moment really dependent on God." Lewis says natural gifts carry a similar danger. If we have intelligence and health and popularity, we are likely to be quite satisfied with our character as it is and not make God part of our lives. The Savior tells us not to place too much value on material things because they are temporary and transitory. The message is simple: if the joy we find is not permanent, then it's made of the wrong stuff.

106

The law of Christ is the law of inner perfection— overcoming weaknesses, motivating ourselves to higher performance. Basic strength comes from obedience, but higher strength comes from inner perfection—perfection of thought and motive, getting the heart in tune. Norman Vincent Peale says he doesn't believe anyone can be emotionally healthy without a sound and vital faith in God: "If you have the feeling that your life has no meaning, you're in a pretty dire way, because that's really a mental and spiritual illness." We need to walk with God and seek his guidance. If we do that, we'll have victories over problems and gain new insights into our lives. And we'll be more apt to feel as the words of the hymn suggest, "Jesus, the very thought of thee with sweetness fills my breast. . . . Nor voice can sing, nor heart can frame, nor can the memory find a sweeter sound than thy blest name, O Savior of mankind."

Spiritual Refueling

Just as the machines of our motorized age come to a halt when they run out of gas, so our spiritual motors shut down when they run out of spiritual fuel. In our troubled world we need to think about refueling ourselves spiritually to make sure we don't run out of this precious energy source.

There is a kind of joy that comes with increased spirituality, and those who have grown most spiritually are those who have become experts in living. Spiritual power brings a capacity to make decisions with greater and greater awareness. It also brings true exhilaration, the incomparable antidote to weariness. Without it, life may seem routine . . . pedestrian . . . and purposeless. This, in turn, brings physical and mental weariness—all of it the result of spiritual slackness.

Research has shown a strong relationship between certain spiritual values—such as the feeling that life has meaning and direction—and happiness. People who lack meaning in their lives tend to be less happy with almost every aspect of life. They are less happy with their financial situations, their homes, their jobs, their marriages, their friends, and even their physical attractiveness.

Life really becomes better only when we become better, and life unfolds only as we unfold spiritually—like flowers unfolding in the sunshine. Things may seem dark at times, but we should never lose our appetite for the true sweetness and light of spirituality. To increase it, we must do as the Savior said: "If any man will come after me, let him deny himself, and take up his cross, and follow me. For . . . whosoever will lose his life for my sake shall find it. For what is a man profited, if he shall gain the whole world, and lose his own soul?" (Matt. 16:24-26.) The Savior didn't mean that we should give up our lives in the literal sense, but that we should lose them in a greater cause, in the cause of spirituality.

We can refuel our spiritual motors by growing closer to the Lord, by reaching out to touch our neighbors, and by coming in daily contact with the principles of spiritual living. As Thomas A. Kempis in *The Imitation of Christ* pointed out, "There is no peace in the heart of a worldly man, who is entirely given to outward affairs, but only in a fervent, spiritual man."

Forgiving

All of us make mistakes. Sometimes we fall short of our best intentions. We are occasionally short-tempered and irritable when we mean to be calm and kind, stingy when we mean to be generous. In fact, life teaches us that to be human is to blunder, to have a marvelous set of ideals in our mind and to live somewhere beneath them.

Since we know that about ourselves, it should be no surprise, then, that others are as fallible as we are. They don't always live up to their best intentions, either. They wrestle with life and at times fail. And sometimes in their shortness of sight, their tremblings under pressure, they may bruise or disappoint us. We are all vulnerable to the pain inflicted by another when he's being less than he means to be. A barbed word may snag our serenity. A criticism may wound us to the marrow. That is when we have one of those rare opportunities to be like the Lord and forgive.

"Father, forgive them; for they know not what they do," uttered the Christ, while still hanging from the cross, and the

Romans, indifferent to His pain, frolicked around him. (Luke 23:34.) Most of us know, too, what it is to be forgiven by the Lord when, from dark feelings, we turn to let his face shine upon us. His forgiveness is like a sweet amnesia. When we turn to him again, he'll remember our weakness no more. In fact, the world he has created seems to echo with the concept. Forgiveness is the intensified fragrance of the flowers we've just crushed within our hands. Forgiveness is the green shoot that struggles up in a charred forest.

But while we understand the Lord's forgiving us, it may seem harder for us to forgive another, especially while we are still smarting under his heel. When we struggle to forgive, it may be time to remember Henry Wadsworth Longfellow's words, "The little I've seen of the world teaches me to look upon the errors of others in sorrow, not in anger." Struggling humanity. How much we need to forgive one another, and what a spiritual lift it is to the torn heart, not only to be forgiven, but to truly learn to forgive.

JESUS
CHRIST

Come

One of the most frequent words in Christ's vocabulary was a small one—*come*. The gestures which we associate with him echo that same idea. Arms outstretched in welcome, his entire being said, "Come." This is not a restricted invitation for the few, for the elect, for those who somehow deserve it; he made it open and for all, no matter how weak or afraid or hesitant. "Come unto me, all ye that labour and are heavy laden," he said, "and I will give you rest." (Matt. 11:28.) At another time, he said, "Suffer little children to come unto me, and forbid them not," appealing to the little child in each of us. (Luke 18:16.) Come follow me, in fact, was the message of his life.

Come. It is an immediate appeal, admitting no excuses. We who say to the Lord, "I am too busy. I am too tired. I will work you in at another time," have missed the point. There is not a mortal being who is not burdened with cares that threaten to absorb him altogether. All are preoccupied, all busy. But when Christ said to Peter and Andrew fishing in the waters of Galilee, "Come . . . , and I will make you . . . fishers of men," they dropped their nets and came. (Mark 1:17.)

Come. It is without qualifications. Not come when we are perfect. Not come when we have no doubts or smudges, when life is uncontested and we have no problems. Nor is it an invitation to come only when life is at its darkest—only in time of dire need. It is a simple, "Come now. Come as you are."

Why is the Lord so insistent about this invitation? Probably because he walked with us and knows firsthand the mysteries, violence, and contradictions of life on this earth. He knows that if we will come to him in pain, we will leave in joy. If we come in confusion, we will leave in clarity. If we come in darkness, we will leave in light. So he offers the invitation and leaves it extended with a kind of divine hopefulness—until we respond.

My Kingdom Is Not of This World

Perhaps the longest hours mortals have ever suffered were those of the Jewish Sabbath just after Jesus Christ was crucified. His disciples scattered, his followers agonized. Where was the Master whose promise had been stronger than Roman tyranny? Where was the Savior whose words had moved them beyond dead tradition? He seemed gone forever.

And to make it harder, on Sunday morning when Mary Magdalene had come with other women to anoint his body with spices, the tomb was empty. It seemed that even his body, this last bit of comfort, had been stolen. Mary did not know that an angel had come in the night and rolled back the stone. She did not comprehend when the same angel told her, "He is not here: for he is risen." (Matt. 28:6.) Neither did Peter and other disciples comprehend the meaning of the slackened grave clothes.

Finally only Mary Magdalene was left, weeping alone in the garden. "Woman, why weepest thou?" asked a voice. Mary was not sure who addressed her, but assuming it was the caretaker she moaned that she did not know where her Lord's body had been taken. "Mary," said the voice, the tones familiar, personal. And then she knew. (See John 20:13-16.)

Now, we might wonder why Mary did not immediately recognize Christ. Were her eyes so cast down with grief that she did not look up when she sensed a person there? We do not know. Perhaps she saw Christ but did not comprehend, just as the disciples heard the message of the resurrection but did not understand.

We today have the same problem. World-weary and tired, our eyes cast down, we do not let him through our misery or self-imposed barriers. "Why weepest thou?" he asks, and thinking it's the caretaker we dismiss the voice. "Whom seekest thou?" he asks, and caught up in ourselves, we hang our heads. Even when he reaches his arms around us, all we sometimes feel is the cold reality of our own frustrations.

We need not wonder that his disciples did not understand the resurrection, that one of his dearest friends did not recognize his voice. Mortality is a time when we become preoccupied and often miss meaning. But his promises are real; his caring penetrates to each individual life. "Mary," he called to one weeping woman in an intimate tone. He calls our name just as clearly.

Back to the Basics

One of the great lessons of life is that all areas of endeavor have their fundamentals, their basic principles that stand as the foundation for knowledge and action. In science, we must turn repeatedly to the basic laws of physics and chemistry. In education, there are the rudiments of language and reasoning that must precede all other learning. The free enterprise system operates upon the basic axiom of supply and demand. This same principle of basics applies to religion as well. Despite the various theologies and diverse claims that characterize the Christian churches of today, we must all return again and again to the basic and fundamental tenet of Christianity: which is that foundation of Jesus Christ.

It is he who is and must be the spiritual cornerstone of Christianity. The Savior, by his own admission, did not come principally as a social reformer, an inspired philosopher, or even as an organizer of religion. His principal mission was that he came as the Son of God, the Redeemer of mankind. This claim makes Christ unique among the world's religious figures. No other individual has so boldly maintained that he alone is "the way, the truth, and the life." (John 14:6.)

Now, we cannot discount Christ's assertion that he was the Son of God and still maintain at the same time that he was only a sublime teacher, a moral leader, a great thinker—for truth is not clothed in deceptions and falsehoods. He could not be both a great leader and dishonest about his divine mission. Either Jesus was what he claimed to be, the Savior of mankind, or he was a great imposter. Thus, whatever we pursue in the name of Christianity—whether it's social reform, charity, or religious instruction—we must recognize Jesus' claim to divine authority. So it is that we must turn again to the fundamental truth of Christian belief. We turn to Christ, the Messiah, the Redeemer of Mankind, even the Son of God.

Do We Despise Him?

Almost two thousand years following the mortal ministry of Jesus Christ, it may be difficult for us to imagine him rejected, to imagine him persecuted and scorned. We revere and worship him and he is worshipped by Christians worldwide for the divinity of his birth, the perfect purity of his life, the remarkable sacrifice of his death, and the hope we have in his resurrection. And yet his coming was prophesied not only as hopeful, but as troubled. Seven hundred years before his birth the prophet Isaiah wrote: "He is despised and rejected of men; a man of sorrows, and acquainted with grief: and we hid as it were our faces from him; he was despised, and we esteemed him not." (Isa. 53:3.)

Surely, we do not despise him. Surely, we have not turned our faces from him. Yet, in his atoning sacrifice, each of our sins has a part. Jesus Christ did not die because of the jealous whim of an apostate clergy, or because an ancient government would not stand against the injustice of his crucifixion. Jesus went to the cross to atone for the sins that separate us from him; to save us, in spite of the ways in which our lives have despised him. Jesus went to the cross for us, even though we may have turned our faces away from him.

Therefore, we must not look to others for examples of betrayal. Surely, we may find the Pilate or the chief priest, the proud and open disdainer of Christ. But it was Christ's chief disciple, Peter, who denied the Savior at the time of his humiliation before the Romans. Just so, there is in each of us who are his modern disciples the moment of failure, the moment of sin and doubt. Christ anticipated these moments when our faces would turn from him, when we would despise him with our lives. He anticipated them; and he died for them.

The prophet Isaiah continues: "He was wounded for our transgressions, he was bruised for our iniquities: the chastisement of our peace was upon him; and with his stripes we are healed." (Isa. 53:5.) The resurrection of Jesus Christ is our guarantee. We are healed, if only we will not turn from him, if only we will not despise him with our lives; if only we will love him and live our lives in harmony with the simple grace and love he brought to the world two thousand years ago.

The Coming

Jesus, who created the world, could certainly have chosen any birthplace here. He must have come to a stable by design. Were there no palaces in Israel? Were there no halls decked with finery that smelled of perfume? Were there no comforts in the country, no soft beds or medical attendants? Almost surely there were, but that was not to be his beginning. Surely he could have come to us in a fiery proclamation, making us tremble at his presence, all flesh kneeling at his arrival. But instead he came in the night, a small baby who cried with hunger and looked for warmth in his mother's arms. We may even wonder that he came to us at all, Immanuel, God with us, instead of a divine and distant being, too high to assume our problems with our pain.

He came, however, not to impress us in the ways with which we are used to impressing each other. Not by opulence or power or distance. He came to look like us and feel with us, bearing our griefs and carrying our sorrow, so that when we kneel at the very limits of our endurance, he knows because he has been there before us. He came to the sick, the great healer whose own body was wounded in the world. He came to the poor, a wanderer who had no home. He came to the forsaken, a man betrayed by a kiss from his friend. He came to the discouraged, a teacher whose followers deserted him at his most critical moment.

He came to all of us with a personal concern and an identity with mortal man. He said, "For I was an hungered, and ye gave me meat: I was thirsty, and ye gave me drink: I was a stranger, and ye took me in." (Matt. 25:35.) His followers asked, "When did we do this?" and he answered that it was when they did it to "the least of these my brethren." (Matt. 25:40.) There is a Christmas lullaby that pleads, "Be near me Lord Jesus; . . . and love me, I pray." It is a plea that is answered even before it is uttered—for we adore him only because he first adored us. And he came quietly to a stable on a silent night to show us just how much.

Jesus Wept

Among the most poignant scriptures to be found in the sacred writings of Christianity is that which is recorded in the gospel of John. A short verse there describes Christ's response to the death of one of his friends. Recorded are these two words: "Jesus wept." (John 11:35.) On that occasion, Jesus shed tears for a single contemporary whom he loved. The event openly displays Christ's capacity to love and feel sorrow for the misfortunes of those around him.

It was not long after this tragedy that Christ faced his own imminent death. Shortly before the crucifixion he went with his disciples to a place called Gethsemane. There in prophetic agony he witnessed the passing of all peoples, of all nations, of us. He discerned that his commandment that we love one another even as he loved us would be largely rejected by mankind. Once, twice, and for a third time he returned to his friends to share the awesome burden; each time he found them asleep. Alone, he took upon himself the sins of the world, suffering for all generations of humanity. And in the depths of that divine despair, he wept.

He wept for the countless unknown soldiers of nameless battles and forgotten wars and for their orphaned children, their widowed wives, their grieving mothers. He wept for the maimed in body and soul who haunt the boweries of large cities, for the aged who wait in nursing homes for visitors who never come, and for the meek and believing who are taken advantage of by the crafty and unscrupulous. He wept because of the ignorance that has made much of mankind live out its life in political and intellectual slavery, and because of superstition that still keeps men in spiritual bondage.

For all of this, and more, the Creator of heaven and earth suffered an exquisite agony. Across the centuries, the lone figure of noble manhood, weeping among the shadows of Gethsemane, looms above humanity. And thus, while his disciples slept, Jesus wept and perhaps still weeps, while mankind sleeps.

HOLIDAYS
AND
SEASONS

A Time to Rejoice

Perhaps our deepest dread is the fear of extinction, of being blown out like a candle flame, of ceasing to be. That inescapable fear of the unknown at times grips each of us, and the more we love life, the more we fear death. That's why Christians everywhere feel a mighty surge of hope on Easter. For millions of people, Easter morning is the most stirring time of the year . . . a time when we are filled with awe and reverence, with wonder and gratitude.

Easter—or more accurately what happened that we commemorate at Easter—removes that fear of extinction. It reaffirms that there is life beyond the grave. Eternal life is a reality, just as much as earth life and bodily death are realities. Christ lives and man shall live. Human history holds no more important and joyful message. The world has never been the same since the resurrection of Christ. This staggering event is the cornerstone of Christianity. To believe in the immortality of individuals is to believe in God, since eternal life without divine guidance is difficult to imagine. Yes, the resurrection does promise a continuation of life, a renewal of relationships. And that gives each of us added purpose. The family and friends, the commitments, the involvements we create in this life will be as immortal as our own souls.

The whole spiritual pattern of the Christian world is interwoven with the wonder of Easter. We need the miracle of Easter in the kind of world in which we live. We need the thrill of it to make us feel God's nearness. It is an adventure in faith and an expression of joy. What greater announcement to the world upon Christ's victory than those three simple words, "He is risen." (Mark 16:6.) That is the great message of Easter—the message that death is not a finality, but a gateway . . . a gate through which we must all travel, a gate that leads to life eternal and the Savior.

The Spirit of Christmas

Christmas is a time for remembering friends, a time for kindness and generosity, but it is often a difficult season because of the challenge of brotherly love in a world filled with hardship, violence, and mistrust. With all the advancements in science and technology, it seems at times we have made little progress in our ability to get along with each other—to love others who live next door, down the street, or on foreign soil. Sometimes it seems 2,000 years have done little to change the world's need for peace and goodwill. But we are willing to try harder during the Christmas season to reaffirm the principles taught by a man known as the Prince of Peace.

The true spirit of Christmas does not require wealth or power. It is best expressed by giving of ourselves through love and kindness, through unselfishness and concern for others. It is when we give of ourselves that we really give, and such an approach to life has a positive effect on the giver. As Charles Dickens said, "No one is useless in the world who lightens the burden of it to anyone else."

Self-taught philosopher Eric Hoffer observed that our capacity for tolerance, for getting along with others, depends in large measure on our capacity for getting along with ourselves. He said, "The self-respecting individual will try to be as tolerant of his neighbor's shortcomings as he is of his own." One of the most important phases of our personal growth is to develop an understanding relationship to others. We are not really mature until we have an ability and a willingness to see ourselves as one among others and to do unto others as we would have them do to us.

124

How is it with each of us? Is our heart in the right place? Does our life encompass a philosophy of service to others? The Savior, whose birth we celebrate this season, made friendship the cornerstone of his life. As recorded in John, the Savior said, "A new commandment I give unto you, That ye love one another; as I have loved you, that ye also love one another. By this shall all men know that ye are my disciples. (John 13:34-35.) This Christmas season, let us be disciples of Christ, let us open our hearts so the spirit of love and brotherhood may enter in. Let us once again rededicate our lives to those principles that offer all the promise of peace.

Were You There?

Were you there on that Christmas night? Many were—citizens of Bethlehem who went about their work and didn't know a child was born. It's not that he wasn't expected. For thousands of years the people had word of his coming, waiting for a Savior; but now, at the moment, it was all so ordinary. A mother, travelworn and weary, her husband with anxious eyes, and a baby who probably looked just like any other. No pomp, no press, no general announcement of his birth. He left his throne of glory to enter in a manger—and he did it quietly.

Those who found him had pulled away from the clamor to do so. The shepherds could hear the angels' chorus because they were not in the jangle of a city. The wise men searched out signs. But most simply overlooked the scene and waited for the King to come in might and glory and to crush the world's oppressions with a stroke. They missed it all. And so might we, all these years later, no wiser than the preoccupied innkeepers when we fail to see his presence in our lives.

That is because, of course, he still comes quietly, without loud proclamations. He does not crush our oppressions with a stroke but takes our hand and walks us through them with the sure experience of one who knows. But maybe, most importantly, though he came to all of us collectively, his ministrations are personal, letting each of us see him just how we need him. To those whose health is impaired, he is the great healer. To the world's forgotten, he is the one who notices even a sparrow's fall. To the frightened, he is the comforter.

For all of us caught in the fog and frustration of mortality, his birth is a reminder that whoever we are and whatever burden we carry, God loves and remembers us. He sent his son into the trials and dust of this earth to tell us so. Therefore, at Christmas time, let us receive this gift of love. Were you there on that Christmas night? No. But our great hope is that, had we been, we would have hurried to the manger to place our gifts and sorrows at his feet. And that invitation to come unto him is still open.

To Know the Christ at Christmas

As dusk turned to darkness on that silent night long ago, the inns of the day were overcrowded. The small towns teemed with travelers and animals, and people plodded down the dusty roads through Bethlehem. For most of them this day and night would be no cause for celebration. In days to come, if they remembered at all, they would note with distaste that they were forced to travel here to pay their taxes to their Roman overlords. Worldly cares hung heavily upon this people as the quiet night came on. But for a handful of humble shepherds in the nearby rocky hills and for a group of searching scholars in a far-off land, this would be a night never to be forgotten.

Why were these few so privileged and not the others? The question is important for each of us as we approach this Christmas, for we could find ourselves in either group. The Rev. Peter Marshall expressed it eloquently when once he prayed, "Forbid it, Lord, that we should celebrate without understanding what we celebrate, or like our counterparts so long ago, fail to see the star or to hear the song of glorious promise." The question is, shall we spend Christmas like those long-ago taxpayers or like the shepherds and the magi?

If we would share the feelings of the shepherds we must be like them. They were humble men, aware of the earth and its seasons. They were kindly men of true compassion, ready to face hardship.

They had a deep respect for God and heaven, so much so that they were "sore afraid" when first the angels came. But they quickly changed their fear to faith when told about the newborn king. (See Luke 2:9-20.) And what of those who traveled from the east to find the one they knew as "King of the Jews"? So different in appearance from the shepherds yet so similar in heart were they whom Matthew calls "wise men." Not clever, crafty, self-important, puffed up in their scholarship—they were more than learned, they were wise. As they offered up their gifts they whispered simply, "We are come to worship him." (Matt. 2:1-2.)

Let us upon this Christmas time resolve to seek and search and see the signs that God has left for us to find him. Let us approach him reverently and kneel as though beside the manger to offer up a silent prayer of thanks to him for sending us his Son. Then we will hear the angels and feel the peace he promised. We will know the Christ at Christmas.

The History Lecture—Thanksgiving, 1621

Today we study a history lesson of ten thousand years: of the species called man we learn; with laws, customs, arts, traditions we become acquainted—clusters of peoples, of men and women like us, being born, giving birth, dying; nations of languages and governments traveling their course. The names change as we turn the pages: Babylonians, Macedonians, the Greeks and Romans, Huns and Mongols. Governments rise and fall, the conquered become the conquerors and then the conquered once again. Fledgling heresies become new truths, and old truths turn to new superstitions in the spiraling cycles of human history.

We are impressed with the sameness of it, the destruction, the ingratitude, the inevitable decay. We see new inventions developed, then witness their employment in the further destruction of human life. Decades and centuries of war pass before our startled eyes. Half hidden, almost obliterated by the catastrophic events of history, wedged between the demise of an old civilization and the birth of a new, brief nova—a single event—in an entire galaxy of human history and memorabilia; turning the pages slowly, we find it.

Plymouth, Massachusetts. The season is fall, the year 1621. A little band of starving pilgrims is there, half their number already dead from disease, hunger, and cold; the few survivors, determined, resolute to remain, to perish if necessary. In their poverty, a feast is held—a simple meal by modern standards: berries and corn bread, venison, wild vegetables and turkey. But more than food was served that day—gratitude and friendship were also shared: gratitude for the freedom to worship, govern, and perhaps die according to the dictates of their own conscience; and friendship for Indian brothers who had helped them survive.

Gratitude, unselfish thanksgiving—not for the felling of cities or the subjugation of enemies but for a bit of corn and ripe squash. We are astonished at the simplicity and quaintness of it, with the grandeur and nobility of it. It raises our spirit, provides new hope in the species, gives us historical evidence of our own divine potential. An unsullied page of smirchless innocence from the diary of mankind, a spiritual banner, waving proudly over humanity: Thanksgiving—a human legacy, not for Plymouth only, nor these United States—but for all places, all peoples, all times.

Learning Appreciation

"A man stood before one of J. M. W. Turner's unrivaled paintings and said, 'I can see nothing in it.' Then the great artist replied, 'Don't you wish you could?'" It is now a season of Thanksgiving, a time—in theory—when we should swell with appreciation. But too many of us eat our turkey with tired taste buds and turn numb eyes to the world. We're too weary to be thankful, or we've let life's miracles become ordinary to us. We have too little time or too many troubles. The reasons abound, but the result is the same: we travel through life as if we've never taken the trip, missing it all.

But the happiest people in the world are not those who have easy days, painless relationships, or lives without loss. The happiest people are those, whatever their lot, who have learned the art of appreciation. They don't expect of the earth what it can't deliver: life without frustration. Instead, they revel in what it can give. Sometimes it takes an eye to see it. Andrew Wyeth once said that the colors beneath a stalk of wheat drove him wild with joy. He said he'd give anything to capture them on canvas.

Writer Hart Crane found such excitement in the English language that he'd search for days for the perfect word for a poem he was writing. One man said he was waiting in the same office with Hart Crane when suddenly Crane let out a roar of jubilation, finding a certain word in a dictionary.

A mother, watching her infant in a baby swing, noticed the child's eyes light up with sudden understanding. The baby thrust his hand forward toward a toy, widely missing the mark, but it was a moment of discovery—the first time he'd ever reached for something. Seeing the miracle of that ordinary step in human development, the mother soared all day.

The colors beneath a stalk of wheat, a word in a dictionary, a baby doing a very usual thing—most of us would not be filled at such moments, but we are the poorer for it. We must learn to see and understand, stop and revel in life's bounteous gifts to us. Feeling appreciation for what we have gives us strength to deal with what we don't have and grants us happiness in the gray days. Let us not stand before the world and say, "I see nothing in it," for the only true reply is, "Don't you wish you could?"

A Day for Reflection

As Memorial Day tributes cause us to reflect about those who have passed on, we should remember that all is well with them, that we are experiencing but a brief separation from them, and that the process of life and death has been designed by a loving Father in heaven. But even with the assurance that life itself does not end, as we know it, the separation of family and friends through mortal death is often a difficult experience. Consider, though, how magnified and tragic the grief must be for those who fail to understand the full purpose of life and death. As J. Reuben Clark said, "The world that is to come after is beyond all comprehension that we have. I think that when we undertake to measure it by the pageantry that we know, we envision scarcely a shadow of the glory of eternity."

Life does have purpose and meaning. And although there are many unanswered questions, they should not be a problem for us because of our knowledge of the resurrection. In a sense, we were born to die. Upon birth, we inherit the seeds of death, but it's not something we should be fearful about. The length of stay does not matter as long as the time has been profitably spent. And it isn't the work we do that's important, but the way we conduct ourselves and the relationship we have with the God who gave us life. On the Judgment Day we won't be asked about the positions we held or the honors and tributes we received. Only the works of our lives and the true intent of our hearts will be judged.

On Memorial Day, millions of Americans make their way to cemeteries and shrines to pay tribute to friends and loved ones. Surely there are moments of sadness as they recall fond memories and associations, as they remember those individuals who have made their lives richer and more meaningful. Memorial Day seems to bring two messages: the message of hope, the realization that life does not end with death but continues beyond the grave; and the message of encouragement to make the most of our relationships each day, to strengthen them, to give and receive from friends and loved ones while we are yet together in this life.

Perhaps the best thing we can do at this time is to reflect on our own future, whatever our age. Where do we go from here? One day we will follow the same path that has been marked for us by those who have already completed their earthly life. Perhaps reflections on Memorial Day will bring perspective into our own lives and encourage us to reexamine our own priorities.

A Tonic for Mankind

"Verdant meadows, stately forest, my heart longing yearns for thee." The text of that song by Handel focuses on the need to show reverence for the miracle of nature. This world is one of the great gifts God has given us. Its beauty is all around us, and to commune with God in the out-of-doors is one of the best remedies for spiritual ills. Nature does her best to feed man. In return, we must be receptive to her charm and allow her to stir our spirits, to show us how we might begin anew. We must prove, as an ancient prophet put it, that we are not past feeling. (See Eph. 4:17-19.)

Surely the unity and complexity of nature are awesome as we observe the workings of the natural world around us. We see not only beauty, but order and harmony as well, as each blossom comes forth. Spring seems to bring out the best in each of us. It is interesting to observe the return to the outdoors after a winter spent inside . . . to observe friendships renewed over backyard fences; to enjoy the fragrances of budding blossoms; to see color return to the earth again; to hear the sounds and see the sights of life being renewed in every form. As we smell the early morning fragrance of spring, we are motivated, we set new goals, we make plans for the summer. It is a time of renewal—a ritual we experience every year. We feel God around us and know of his goodness.

Often in our urbanized life of deadlines and overcrowded days, of space-age stresses and the ever-increasing quest for material things, we overlook God's great gift to us and to our souls . . . the calming salve of the natural world. Nature does speak to the spirit. Regular contact with nature—a few quiet moments with animals and fields, with trees and birds, with a warm sun and clear skies—can have an almost miraculous effect on our beings. It can strengthen us and give us confidence to work through difficulties. And not unexpectedly, it often returns us to faith and reason.

A Season for Reflection

Summer is an ideal season for mental, emotional, and spiritual tune-ups. Just as a finely tuned engine needs adjustments to run most efficiently, so our lives run more efficiently if we take time for needed adjustments and improvements. During the course of a year, habit often dulls the edge of observation. Our actions become routine and our behavior patterns stay so close to us that our angle of vision no longer provides an accurate perspective on ourselves.

That's why vacations, weekend trips, overnight campouts, and other summer activities with our families help us to see ourselves more clearly. We begin to take a fresh and careful look at ourselves. The summer breaks from our daily routines, regardless of their length, can often tell us more about ourselves and the areas in which we need improvement than months of self-examination at home.

Summer evenings also provide a reflective opportunity to get to know ourselves better. As we watch the beauty and order of nature around us, we realize that proper self-management is a great virtue . . . that it leads to personal pride, which is a great motivator. We realize that self-management through self-discipline develops integrity and the ability to be more honest with God, with our families, and with our friends. And as we help a neighbor with a summer project, we understand what the Savior meant when he said, "It is more blessed to give than to receive." (Acts 20:35.) That advice is not mere moralizing but an absolute psychological law for maintaining mental and emotional health.

Finally, we would suggest that there is no better season than summer for fine-tuning ourselves spiritually, because we often tend to let our commitment and enthusiasm for religious matters wither in the summer fun. As C. S. Lewis has suggested, Satan undermines our spirituality by using our summer desires to get us away from religion. So summer is a time to keep our religious guard up and strengthen ourselves and our families' spirituality . . . a time to remember that the rewards and blessings offered by the Lord are more important than all the world's pleasures. In fact, this is a good time to renew our dedication to him who gave us *all* our seasons.

Seeing Spring

In springtime, the world is renewed. The crocuses put forth their shoots in search of the sun; the grasses that were gray beneath the snow turn green again; the snow itself, which only yesterday was ice-packed in the mountains, becomes a life-giving river to valley farms being plowed in preparation for the season's planting. For those who believe, the miracle of spring's regeneration is also a witness of God. In spring, death surrenders to life; and all the resurrections of the season reveal a world more abundant, more hopeful, more certain than we may have remembered.

But the evidence of God's love and plan are not only apparent in the season but also in each of us. We are just witnesses to the truth of spring, but our lives are renewing testimony of the God who gave them. Isn't it a paradox, then, that many of those same people whose lives testify of God do themselves deny him? Many people look at spring and do not see a divine plan but see the mere working of change, the random association of some natural selection. How strange that the handiwork should deny the hand, that the created should deny the creator. How incredible that men should look on spring and not see in it the miracle of God's creation and the hope of his salvation.

When God made us to be his children, he also made us to be free—free to choose. So it is that we may choose to see, to believe, to hope . . . or to be blind, to ignore, to doubt. Spring is as beautiful for the unbeliever as the believer. The sun is as warm, the days as bright. But, for those who see in spring the power of resurrection and salvation, that same sun is even more welcome. Because, for the believer, the hope of spring shines in every moment, is present in every opening flower and greening field. We see Christ all around us and the power of God's love in every movement. We see a world in which all the creatures are creations of our God; and, we know this season, this spring, is a testimony of him.

The Message of Spring

Yes, awake, thou wintry earth. Fling off thy sadness . . . renew thy bright array with fairest blooms of spring. Ah, the sights and sounds and smells of spring—the shimmer of dancing rain . . . the aroma of fresh turned soil . . . the promise of pink in an apricot bloom . . . the glint of morning sunlight on the window sill. No wonder we feel increased vigor each morning.

Spring draws us deeper into that mysterious and universal stream we call life. We eagerly await this joyful season because of the profound message it sends about the eternal process of self-renewal and recommitment. Each year we watch the ritual of spring, and we learn more about our own natural growth processes, about our own need to revitalize, about our own potential for development.

Just as there is a reawakening in the world around us, so there is a reawakening within each of us. We feel a new attentiveness that heightens every experience. We yearn to reach out to others . . . to consider new ideas . . . to develop inner resources. And as we enlarge our human horizons, we find that old challenges become new opportunities, just as old trees push forth new branches. When spring fever strikes, we traditionally clean out our homes and let the fresh breezes blow through open windows. So too can we open the windows of our lives to the fresh breezes of new beginnings, new friendships, new dedication.

The message of spring is just that simple—the fresh breezes of new beginnings. It is a message of renewal. Our talents, our intelligence, our happiness are never lost. They may rest for a period as a tree rests for the winter, but they are ever renewable as the spring bud renews the twig. The warm sunshine of faith, the fresh rain of encouragement, the bright light of purpose . . . that's all it takes for our personal renewal, for our personal spring. That's the simple message of the season. Let us give thanks for the divine origin of this wonderful elixir—spring—provided for us by a loving God.

The Workmanship of Mine Hands

One of life's more youthful and exciting times is the annual renewal of the earth called spring. It's a time when one can have a simple but powerful communion with nature. It is one of the best remedies for spiritual ills. It stirs our spirits. We experience surges of energy and optimism as we witness longer periods of sunlight, warming temperatures, and the landscape putting on a new face of color. But the miracle of spring comes so quietly each year that many of us take it for granted and fail to comprehend its significance.

Spring, it seems, is a season more than any other to reassure us that there is a God in the heavens. Emerson said, "All I have seen teaches me to trust the Creator for all I have not seen." And the Lord said to Moses, "I will show thee the workmanship of mine hands." (Moses 1:4.) Surely to observe the glories of nature is to verify the existence of God. Another scripture reads, "all things denote there is a God; yea, even the earth and all things that are upon the face of it . . . do witness that there is a Supreme Creator." (Alma 30:44.)

Who can look upon a tulip in bloom, a budding cherry blossom, who can smell a fresh lilac tree or the air after a gentle rain and not ponder the power that can compose and orchestrate the beautiful rebirth of an entire landscape? All of God's creations bear witness of his existence—including the earth, moon, and stars. As one spiritual leader said, "Any man who hath seen any or the least of these hath seen God moving in his majesty and power." (D&C 88:47.)

So, as spring makes its debut, let us use the beauty of the season to commune with God and give thanks for this annual miracle, for another of the great gifts he has given us. Regular contact with nature, especially in the springtime, can have a renewing effect on our dispositions and personalities. It can strengthen us and give us confidence to work through difficulties. And, not unexpectedly, it often returns us to faith and reason. As we hear in the lyrics of the song by Handel, "Verdant Meadows," let spring be more than just another season; let's "let thy beauty now remind me of thy God, ever gracious, mighty ruler over all."

Autumn's Special Message

With its brilliant colors and bountiful harvests, autumn is a season of pure poetry. It is the fullness of all seasons—triumphantly grown old, rich and fulfilled. It penetrates the inner universe of the soul as we witness its message of mortality . . . as we see the falling red and yellow-gold leaves . . . the trees increasingly bare . . . as we become aware of the fading warble of birds and the absent chirp of crickets. In autumn we are keenly aware of parallels between nature and our own later years. Autumn's quiet and effortless transformation from summer is so gradual that it escapes daily observation. So too must we yield ourselves naturally to the rhythm of the years and let our own inner timetables complete their important cycles.

Seneca tells us to embrace old age and love it, for "the gradually declining years are among the sweetest in a man's life; . . . even when they have reached the extreme limit, they have their pleasure still." The trick to living longer, it is said, is to think older when we are young so we can act younger when we are old. Almost all people who reach their eighties or nineties in good health follow this basic formula. As with the autumn season, the later years can be the most beautiful and interesting . . . the most exciting and rewarding. A noted gerontologist says those people who die with a thousand unfilled dreams are probably the happiest people during their older years.

The autumn harvest also reminds us of Paul's admonition, "Whatsoever a man soweth, that shall he also reap." (Gal. 6:7.) Whatever we have planted through life, we reap in later years. If we have planted the habits of good health, we are more likely to harvest well-being and a long life. If we have planted the bonds of close family ties, the harvest brings joy through all our years. If we have planted the seeds of true friendship, we reap the benefits while sharing autumnal beauty and peace of mind. If we have planted a tiny seed of faith early enough, it has taken root and has grown to become a towering tree that shadows over us and that provides us with everlasting peace of mind. The real comfort of faith comes most reassuringly to those who have planted it early and nurtured it well. So autumn is not only the season of beauty, the season of harvest, the season of poets. For those who have prepared well, it is also the season of fulfillment.

USING
TIME
WISELY

Time for Ourselves

Life is a serious matter. It's a time to learn, a time to progress, a time of purpose. The Lord doesn't want every little thing to get us down. He expects us to be tough, to be emotionally strong. Some individuals seem to have developed a greater capacity than others to cope with life. The closer we become to our Creator, the clearer our perspective will be, the greater our joy, the more manageable our challenges. The scriptures tell us that we "must press forward with a steadfastness in Christ, having a perfect brightness of hope." (2 Ne. 31:20.) We need to be positive and confident. We must create mental expectations about life, about our futures, about ourselves.

Perhaps those who have an easier time with life have invested in their inner space and have developed it to a higher degree. These are the people who have simplified their lives. They search for regular periods of solitude. They take the time to commune with themselves and to come to an understanding of what duties and priorities should be emphasized in their lives. Anne Morrow Lindberg observed in *Gift from the Sea*, "There is a quality to being alone that is incredibly precious. Life rushes back into the void, richer, more vivid, fuller than before." Later she added, "When one is a stranger to oneself then one is estranged from others too. If one is out of touch with oneself, then one cannot touch others."

It is unfortunate that sometimes we must apologize for wanting to be alone, as if it were a secret vice. We should treat ourselves to the benefits of solitude on a regular basis. It isn't difficult. We can begin by scheduling at least fifteen minutes a day, preferably longer, to be alone. A good time is early in the morning when we are refreshed and our minds are clear. There should be no review of the day's activities, no worries about events that lie ahead—simply a few minutes of solitude for introspection. Being at peace with ourselves is critical, for spiritual harmony within quickly translates to outer harmony. Even in the midst of life's troubles and challenges, we will find that the person who has well-developed inner space remains wholly at peace, trusting in God and not in the world.

A Hurried World

We live in a hurried world where there never seems to be quite enough time. The days and weeks melt behind us as we rush through life frantic and breathless. We like our food fast and our stops quick, and if there is any way to cram more into our days as we would into a too-full suitcase, we try. We tell ourselves that when this pressure has passed, this job is finished—then we'll slow down and live.

We've even learned to hurry our children. One of the first questions we ask a youngster is "What are you going to be when you grow up?" We spend their first few years preparing them to read to do well in school. During elementary years we have an eye on getting them ready for high school, and in high school we worry about college. The push is always for tomorrow.

Yet in a very real sense, it is only the present moment that is ours. Tomorrow never comes, for when it is upon us, it has become today with all the pressure and immediacy. If we wait for a mythical tomorrow, when we don't live fully in the present moment, we may find that we miss it all. As Richard L. Evans said, "This is life—and it is passing. What are we waiting for?" Time rushes onward, silent and unresting. Nothing is swifter or more relentless. If we are too hurried today to live as we want to, there are no guarantees that tomorrow will be different.

Joseph Addison observed, "Though we seem grieved at the shortness of life in general, we are wishing every period of it at an end. The minor longs to be of age, then to be a man of business, then to make up an estate, then to arrive at honors, then to retire." And then, we would add, to be young again. Today is the only day we have, and once it has gone we can never have it back. If we run so quickly that it blurs before us, perhaps we need to consider why we run. Maybe it's time to realize there is more to life than increasing its speed.

Lessons of Time

If history can teach us anything, perhaps it is modesty about who we are and what we are. What seems permanent from the vantage of a single life caught in the present is as transient as the wind that erodes a desert city. Institutions and the people who create them burn bright for their moment and then flicker and fail. Haughty pharaoh who once strode Egyptian palaces wildly dreaming of conquest is now just bones in the earth. Sumeria, Babylonia, and Persia, whose soldiers shook the world, are only so much dust. And excessive South American jungles have buried entire cities out of memory. Yes, man has less control here than he wants, far less time than he dreams. He acts his part intensely, believing he is all—and then is gone.

Even a glimpse at our personal history teaches us how time moves us on from who we were. The long days of school that seemed to last forever come and go. When we visit school again we have changed, and the cheers we hear in the halls are only echoes of the past. The football hero has moved on to sell insurance; the prom queen now has wrinkles. Time, which seemed to stand still, did not keep its promise, and we look back from the mirror with older eyes than we remembered. The poet Shelley said it this way, "We are as smoke that drifts above the vale / Whose ever changing shape the breezes tend."

Now, all of this is not to make us despair but to give perspective. Time in its relentlessness will push us on from any heartache. The most intense sorrow, the most agitating anger will soon be but a memory. Life's hurry and impermanence must teach us, too, to be less eager to embrace the current thought, less willing to sell our security for the latest model, less impressed by those who seem high-style. Today's styles, gadgets, and thought will be tomorrow's antiques. The goals we suffer for may in retrospect be just so much trivia. So in these moments here let us evaluate the pull of the present with a wise distance, let us put our hearts on what will not fade, and finally let us love what we love with more intent. The moment will not come again.

Appearance and Reality

One of the themes running through Shakespeare's work is the conflict of appearance and reality. He was the first to tell us that "all that glitters is not gold," and he also reminded us that "every cloud engenders not a storm." In trying to tell us that things are not always as they seem, the bard said, "Things sweet to taste prove in digestion sour."

It is sometimes good for us to reflect on the themes of great literature because their truth isn't always limited to a certain time or people. And we, much more than the people of Shakespeare's day, are living in a world of false images where reality is hard to sort out from appearance. It's a world where a political candidate's hairstyle may prove more important to his campaign than his stand on the issues. It's a world where we know each other so superficially that for some of us our best friends are those flickers of color on a television set. It's a world where our dream homes are the slim facades of a Hollywood movie set, a world where we put on fronts because we are uncertain that people will like us without our veneer.

The great danger in all this is that we may become so confused between appearance and reality that we put our faith and time in the temporary rather than in the eternal, spending a lifetime chasing cotton-candy realities. It is too easy to equate the importance of a person with his visibility, the meaning of a job with its notoriety. We may let those things that seem the most pressing pull us away from the things that are the most important. We may begin to think that power is wealth and influence, rather than personal integrity. It was Kipling who said, "Lo, all our pomp of yesterday / Is one with Nineveh and Tyre," two cities that have utterly vanished from the map.

Appearance and reality—if only they would label themselves so we could clearly recognize them and act accordingly. But appearance has a way of seeming immediate, important, demanding. And reality dressed in simple clothes fades quietly into the background. We rarely have time to stop in our running and ask, "What really matters in the eternal scheme of things?" Thus, there is the father who misses his child's first piano recital but not his business meeting. There is plenty of time for a mindless magazine but not for the scriptures. We learn to envy those who are served and not those who do the serving. Nevertheless, one day when our eyes are clear, appearance with all of its false gaiety and self-seeking will take a final curtain bow, and reality will take its rightful place—center stage. Then we will know if we have put our faith and time in their proper place.

Time for What Is Important

We live in a busy world. There are so many things to do, so many responsibilities pulling for our attention. Even our technologies do not seem able to make our lives less crowded; as soon as we invent a system to simplify one task, another responsibility moves in to consume whatever time we've saved. It may be true that we get more things done by making more efficient use of our time, but it may also mean that as our lives become full, more complex, more detailed, some of the more important aspects of living receive less attention or are forgotten altogether.

For instance, how many times have we justified the amount of time spent away from families, justified the neglect families suffer because of careers or other distractions? "I'm doing these things for you," neglected families are often told. And in fact, while that may be true, it does not make the neglect any less real. Recently, when a boy received such an explanation from his father, who never had time to play ball with him, the boy responded, "The trouble, Dad, is that I'm not in your book."

"Book?" the father asked. "What book?"

"You know," the boy replied, "the book you write your appointments in, the one where you keep track of meetings with important people. I'm not in there."

Jesus spoke about this problem—the problem of mismanaged priorities. The occasion was when he visited the home of Martha, sister to Lazarus and Mary. While Mary sat at the feet of Christ, learning of salvation, Martha worked in the kitchen and was annoyed that Mary did not help her. Finally, Martha complained to Jesus, who answered, "Martha, Martha, thou art careful and troubled about many things: but one thing is needful: and Mary hath chosen that good part, which shall not be taken away from her." (Luke 10:41-42.)

Too often, we do not recognize what is "needful," what is most full of need. Too often, perhaps, we allow what is important in our lives to be displaced by the details and activity that we think we're doing for our families. Someone needs to do the dishes; the details must be taken care of. But sometimes the details can wait so that the words of the Savior may be heard, so that a father will have time to play ball with his son, so that a mother will have time to talk to her daughter, so that what is important receives the most attention in our lives.

More Stately Mansions

We have all seen the remarkable construction of the chambered seashell—how each year the developing marine animal adds another compartment to its home, making a larger, expanded dwelling to accommodate the annual growth. Oliver Wendell Holmes's observation of this phenomenon led him to a conclusion about man's own need for continued growth and development. Speaking of the chambered nautilus, he wrote:

> Thanks for the heavenly message brought by thee,
>   Child of the wandering sea. . . .
> Build thee more stately mansions, O my soul,
>   As the swift seasons roll!
>   Leave thy low-vaulted past!
> Let each new temple, [be] nobler than the last.

The poet's suggestion that we build more stately mansions for our souls, that we continually seek opportunities to progress, is more appropriate today than at any time in the past. Affluence, along with the reduced work week, have provided us with a new freedom—freedom that could be used to explore, to study, to challenge our bodies, our minds, and our spirits.

Unfortunately, however, the vast majority of us will use this free time and means in the pursuit of leisure and recreation. Not that it is unimportant—for we need recreation. Certainly entertainment fills a needed role in our lives; but so do the other aspects of life. Physical, intellectual, and spiritual growth do not always result from passive amusement. Despite this fact, our beaches and resorts are crowded on weekends, while churches that beautify the American landscape remain largely unfilled; and at the same time that literally millions are patronizing less challenging pursuits, there are adult education and evening classes being cancelled for want of interest.

In our effort to derive more and more pleasure from our freedom, many of us have forgotten that lasting happiness cannot occur without growth—growth that is achieved only through challenge and struggle. May we resolve from this moment to use our freedom to expand our personalities; may we exert the time and discipline to gain some new skill, to think some new thought, to achieve some new spiritual insight; may the unfolding of each new moment find us with more stately mansions for our souls.

On Wasting a Lifetime

Is there really, somewhere, in a meadow far away, still a shepherdess who sings all day while she watches her flocks? If there is, we are separated from her by a thousand cares, our world caught up in crisis, strung with personal tensions and responsibilities that tie us up and bind our songs within our hearts. For too many of us the world is bleak and gray and cold, and we are breathless with hurry as we rush from one job to another, with no time for meadows or easy songs.

Before we know it, ten days have passed and then a hundred, and we have not done anything that matters. We have not once touched the world, and it has not touched us. Who is it that winds us up and makes us run and keeps us from the soul of things? A century ago Henry Thoreau observed, "If a man walks in the woods for love of them, half of each day, he is in danger of being regarded as a loafer; but if he spends his whole day as a speculator shearing off those woods and making earth bald before her time, he is esteemed as an industrious and enterprising citizen."

So it is. To fit somebody else's idea of significance, we mold our days, our senses becoming ever so gradually deadened. We watch life dribble away, leak out, and go. But now, before it is gone—now is the time to ask those crucial questions, "Am I living without regrets? If I had today to do over again would there be any changes?"

One writer, Maurine Ward, said this: "If I had it to do again, I'd remember that childhood is short, only a blink long, and I'd leave the cobwebs in the corners to go play with someone small whom I loved. If I had it to do again, I'd remember that my personal allotment of sunsets is numbered, and I'd often take time to watch one before they were all gone. If I had it to do again, I'd care less that the house was perfect and more that my relationships were.

"I'd buy a morning off with a dear one instead of a new couch. I'd sleep when I was tired, hold my tongue when I had an eloquent, angry speech, and pray like I meant it. . . . If I had it to do again." But none of us ever have it to do again, so we must do today the things we would. We must make our life by what we love. To choose anything else is, in the end, to have chosen nothing at all.

AGING

The Best of Life

When we were young, most of us were admonished by our parents to eat our vegetables before the dessert. As adults, we are counseled to put business before pleasure. Most of our accomplishments follow this pattern. We put the time, the effort, the expense into a project, and then we reap the rewards and benefits. Those are the rules of life, we are told. But sometimes it seems life doesn't follow its own rules.

Sometimes it seems the best parts of life come first. Early on, we have a healthier body and perhaps a more beautiful face and form. We enjoy the excitement and challenge of youth. We have what seems like endless years to accomplish our wildest dreams. Nothing is beyond the realms of our aspirations. It is as though we were having our dessert first in life.

Then the responsibilities begin to press more heavily upon us. At the same time, our physical strength begins to slacken. Our skin begins to wrinkle, our eyes may dim, and our ears lose their keen hearing. Our goals and dreams slide further and further beyond our reach. We become conscious of our ever-present limited mortality. Finally, we begin to acknowledge that some of the dreams of our youth may never be realized. Suddenly, it seems we are older. Is it true that in life we have the best first, followed by a gradual decline in accomplishment and fulfillment—a gradual decay and a desolation?

At first glance, this would seem to be the case. And surely it would be if all life offered were the passing amusements of youth.

Fortunately that is not all life has to offer, or even the best of it. There are joys and satisfactions that can only be savored by the senior citizens among us: the fulfillment of a job well done, a career honorably completed; the satisfaction of using our experience to help others along their way; the hand clasp of friends we know are true because they have been tested; the deep love that can only come to people who have weathered many winters together.

So, if some morning we peer into the mirror at a new wrinkle or say good-bye to an old hairline, we may nurse a moment of nostalgia. That is only natural. But this can be replaced by a deep, soul satisfaction that we are learning lessons and building character that can only come from years of living. These are the deepest and richest joys this world has to offer. As Job said so many centuries ago, "With the ancient is wisdom; and in length of days understanding." (Job 12:12.) If we achieve wisdom and understanding from our years on earth, our years will have been well spent, profitable, satisfying, and sweet to us.

The Art of Staying Young

The unforgiving ticking of the clock moves us on—dispassionately, uncontrollably carrying us toward maturity and old age. There is nothing we can do to alter time or impede its progress. We will never be as young again as we are this moment. Despite our best efforts, time soon has its way, revealing the years that measure our lives.

But there are parts of us that age can never mar—indeed, parts of us that grow young with time, become more graceful, less feeble; more perfect, less infirm. For while the body slowly withers and atrophies, the soul rejuvenates with time. This, then, is the art of staying young: to cherish and maintain enthusiasm of the spirit with charity and tenderness of heart, through constant searching and inquiry, by contemplation and appreciation.

To be young at any age is to be young at heart; it is to be reborn every morning in gratitude for our own existence and to be baptized each day in the waters of experience and increased knowledge. To be young is to understand the enduring value of friends and quiet discussions and the fleeting nature of material possessions; it is to trade fashion for grace, inexperience for wisdom, vanity for self-confidence; it is to see ourselves, finally, as we are seen and to understand at last that character and charity are the only investments that pay true dividends.

To have a youthful soul is to find our own lost youth in the eyes of children and grandchildren or to experience true love in the sacred clasp of time-worn hands between lifelong companions. The young refresh themselves in memories of home and past friends and find eternal life in their own resurrection in the fragrant blossom of a lilac bush. Old age follows youth as night the day, but accompanied by its own youthful grace and fascination, still wanting to know, less likely to doubt, more willing to love.

Observations on Aging

Autumn, with its brilliant colors and bountiful harvests, is returning to the northern hemisphere. Autumn is the fullness of all seasons, a time when we are keenly aware of parallels between nature and our own later years. When the fall equinox occurs in our own lives, it would be well to remember that old age is far more than white hair and wrinkles. The true evil is not the weakening of the body but the indifference of the soul. As we grow older, it is more the desire to act than the power to do so that is lost.

"What's the use?" is a dangerous phrase. After having said that, the next question could be, "What's the use of going out?" Then, "What's the use of leaving my room?" And finally, "What's the use of living?" Compare that attitude to that of Pablo Casals. When he was 95, a young reporter asked him, "Mr. Casals, you are 95 years old and the greatest cellist that ever lived. Why do you still practice six hours a day?" Mr. Casals answered, "Because I think I'm making progress." That's quite a different attitude from those who think life is over at 65.

There is also a spiritual side of aging. Life is richer for those who have developed a religious faith to help them through the stresses and trials of everyday living. People who believe in God seem to be more optimistic. They live with increasing commitment as they advance in years. Faith gives us peace and assurance, especially in later years. In today's world, there are many who have wandered from the path of peace, who throng the downward road and reject the wisdom from above. As Thomas A. Kempis pointed out in *The Imitation of Christ*, "True peace of heart can be found only in resisting the passions, not by yielding to them. There is no peace in the heart of a worldly man, who is entirely given to outward affairs; but only in a fervent, spiritual man."

David O. McKay made a similar observation: "If you have lived true to the promptings of the Holy Spirit, and continue to do so, happiness will fill your soul. If you vary from it, and become conscious that you have fallen short of what you know is right, you are going to be unhappy even though you have the wealth of the world." That's because we reap what we sow. Living a virtuous life, being true to ourselves, adhering to sound principles, investing in our families—these are the things that will bring joy and happiness to us in later years. "For where your treasure is, there will your heart be also." (Matt. 6:21.)

The Myths of Aging

It takes a lot of trust in the Lord as we go through life. There are many myths about growing old. Some fear old age. They fear it as a time when they will be alone, bored, useless, and ill. But old age is not that way for most people. The majority of persons beyond retirement age consider life satisfying and definitely worth living.

Researchers find that old age doesn't bring many surprises. People who are well adjusted in middle age tend to be well adjusted during the golden years. And there is a certain exhilarating freedom that comes with senior citizen status. It is no longer necessary to strive for professional recognition. These individuals have earned a chance to relax, to savor life, and to do some of the things they want to do.

Enduring to the end, as God has instructed, does not mean simply lying back and doing nothing. It means continuing to set goals, to work, and to contribute insight, perspective, and experience. A wise observer once said that too often in aging, people do things for the last time and not for the first time. If we reverse that process, that is, try it for the first time at whatever age, we will have an effective antidote against growing old.

Here are a few more thoughts to ponder: First, make plans for the future—long-range, long-term goals along with plans for today and tomorrow. Second, exercise can accomplish wonders. And remember the heart, like the body, also needs exercise. There is nothing more stirring than two elderly people in love, each still finding in the other those qualities that were admired in youth. Third, as we grow older, we become aware of how little we know, and with this awareness comes again the child's sense of wonder—but with increased powers of judgment and discrimination.

Religious faith can also enrich our lives and help us through the stresses of everyday living, whether we are young or old. If we have developed faith in God, we are likely to have faith in others and, most important, in ourselves. Faith in ourselves gives us peace and assurance that we will overcome difficulties and reach the goals of our lives. Those people who leave earth with a thousand unfilled dreams are probably the happiest older people during their later years. They are controlled not by myths of aging, but by the realities of living.

A Time for Self-Renewal

If spring is identified with youth and winter with the senior years, then summer must surely be the time of midlife. We hear a great deal about something called the midlife crisis—that very real psychological transition between youth and middle age. No one escapes it. But the process is not permanent, and it can provide a unique opportunity for self-discovery, renewal, and fulfillment. This crisis doesn't have to mean chaos or disaster, and it doesn't have to leave permanent scars. But it does mean change. Life will not be the same afterward.

For realists, the early signs of restlessness and anxiety are short-lived. Some people, though, spend their entire lives trying to work through the problems, and society's youth cult intensifies the frenzy. Some men trade in old homes and habits for new ones.

Some women look for wrinkle creams and surgery. But mature individuals celebrate their age with enthusiasm, with delight and pride. They don't engage in the desperate race to keep the particular excellences of youth. Our looks may change, and a few character lines may appear, but if we have used our minds and bodies to their fullest, our mental, physical, and spiritual vigor should not diminish.

For most people, the midlife transition is simply a matter of recognizing and acknowledging the inevitable. Many come out of this period feeling better about themselves, their lives, and their work. A great sense of calmness sets in, and extraordinary productivity takes place. At this stage of life, we are usually more in charge of our own lives than ever before. We are more acquainted with our moods, and we can react less emotionally to the moods of others. And there is the relaxing realization that so many problems aren't worth worrying about because they'll shortly be replaced by others, often more interesting.

People who survive the middle years best are those who, in psychiatric language, have good ego strength—people who like and enjoy themselves. And the most fortunate individuals have also discovered the need for God and religion in their lives. They have found that drinking from the life-sustaining water of Christ's well will ease the problems of middle age . . . or any age.

PATRIOTISM

A Responsibility to Our Forefathers

In 1775, during the Second Revolutionary Convention in Virginia, a Virginia farmer rose to tell his countrymen, "I know not what course others may take, but, as for me, give me liberty or give me death." Liberty, as expressed here by Patrick Henry, means the freedom to worship as we please, to speak and read without fear. It means the self-direction each one of us enjoys over our affairs—the choice of schooling, the choice of jobs, the choice of political party. It means the freedom to alter the government as citizens may desire at election time. One U.S. president, Harry S Truman, said, "Liberty does not make all men perfect, nor all society secure, but it has provided more solid progress and happiness and decency for more people than any philosophy of government in history."

Central to the whole fabric of our free society is the thread that runs through it all—the Constitution, a document creating a system of government that has endured the most traumatic events and tests. The U.S. Constitution guarantees freedom and liberty for the individual. Our early forefathers believed freedom and liberty were basic to an individual's development and happiness. They were also convinced that each person has an obligation to society, a responsibility to assist with the machinery that helps guarantee freedom and liberty.

One such responsibility is to assist in the selection of government and community leaders, a responsibility the framers of the Constitution would not have us take lightly, a responsibility envied by countless other nations. It is through our participation in the election process that we validate the sacrifices of so many individuals throughout our country's brief history. Said Thomas Paine, "Those who expect to reap the blessings of freedom must undergo the fatigue of supporting it."

America is the only nation on earth deliberately created in behalf of an idea. That idea was liberty. The goal, above all, was to be free. Our Declaration of Independence proclaimed that purpose. The Constitution was written to assure it. We should never forget that original purpose and never take our liberty for granted.

The Blessing of Freedom

People arriving in the New York harbor by sea are greeted by the majestic Statue of Liberty, her torch raised high in a symbolic salute to freedom. Millions more have visited that national monument to be reminded of the freedom of these United States and the love we have for it. When Americans say we love our country, we mean not only the beauty of its hills, prairies, mountains, and seas, but the love of an inner light in which freedom lives and in which an individual can draw the breath of self-respect.

Living in America is a blessing worth thinking about frequently, not just during the national holidays set aside for that purpose. It is a privilege many people throughout the world would be honored to share. This is the only nation on earth deliberately created not on the basis of geography, but in behalf of an idea. And the idea was liberty, the right to be free. Our Declaration of Independence proclaims it. The Constitution was written to guarantee it. Curiously, few Americans now recall that original purpose, and that means our liberty is too often taken for granted.

The fiber of our nation is strong, but the lessons of history should teach us that freedom is the most easily lost of man's possessions, that apathy is our greatest problem. No nation can endure without the support, dedication, and the enthusiasm of its people. We can fight apathy by remembering the blessings and privileges that come with citizenship, by expressing them openly, and by helping our children understand and appreciate these blessings. We should also have a spirit of godliness, for God and church have always been at the center of activity in America, tying family, community, and nation together.

Ultimately, nations are only as strong as their ideas. When a nation no longer represents an idea, its future is in doubt. Many citizens of the United States have affluence and prosperity, but show a tendency to attribute those conditions solely to personal achievement. That attitude can produce a dangerous pride, a hardness of heart, a false sense of self-sufficiency. Do we really have a right to take our comfort, prosperity, and security for granted when so much of the world lives with anguish, poverty, and fear? No!

The torch of freedom is held high by the Statue of Liberty. Our task is to keep the torch always burning to symbolically illuminate that stirring inscription at the base of the statue: "Give me your tired, your poor, your huddled masses yearning to breathe free. . . . Send these, the homeless, tempest-tossed, to me: I lift my lamp beside the golden door!"

The Price of Patriotism

It's oft been said—and quite truthfully—that freedom is not free, that its price is eternal vigilance, that it must be purchased by each succeeding generation. It is also true that there is a price for patriotism. To love our country and people well, we must learn to serve and sacrifice for them. Now, it is a law of nature that the things for which we struggle hardest are the things we treasure the most. No one learns this lesson better than the pioneers of any endeavor. They are the ones who can appreciate so much only because they give so much. In this context, we are particularly mindful of the American pioneers who trekked across the Western plains; the ardent patriots who settled in the Western valleys of the mountains.

It would have been so easy for them to be bitter. Driven from their homes because of their beliefs, they sought refuge in a land that no one else wanted. The land of sun and sand and sagebrush surrounded by the towering mountains was a difficult and dangerous obstruction to travelers on their way to more easy, fertile country. But to those pioneers, it was their promised land and they treated it as such. In the dusty soil, they saw potential life. On barren plains, their inward vision pictured fields and orchards, groves and gardens. Along each canyon stream, they saw a city. Theirs was the vision—the dream—that is part of every pioneer.

But they did more than dream. They worked, and prayed, and hoped. And as they did, they sang an invitation to whoever would join them in their pursuit. "Come, come, ye Saints," they sang, "no toil nor labor fear." But fearful was the journey. The trail was rough and rutted. More than 6,000 died along the way. Yet those who struggled on took courage in their faith in God and comforted each other with the reassurance that "All is well."

Those pioneers paid the price of patriotism and freedom, and for it they received the rewards that only they could fully appreciate. They prized their freedom and newfound homeland more than life itself. And because they did they loved it, cared for it, and sacrificed for it. Eventually those barren plains became fruitful fields. Today one can stand on a surrounding mountaintop and, with some sense of gratitude to those who perhaps loved it best, praise the effort that made it so. Indeed, we can—as the mountains themselves seem to do—shout for joy for those early pioneer patriots.

Being a Patriot

As America once again celebrates its nationhood, on this anniversary of the signing of the Declaration of Independence, our thoughts return to those early patriots, to those brave men and women who saw past the security of the moment toward the peace of the future. Our debt to all of them, and to the many patriots, both known and unknown, who have sacrificed life and the pursuit of happiness during the proud history of America is eternal. Our gratitude as their beneficiaries must extend beyond the picnics, the barbecues, and the firework displays; it can only be returned in kind: sacrifice for sacrifice, contribution for contribution, our own patriotism in payment for theirs. Thus, patriotism is not the right of the few but the responsibility of the many. It is a moral imperative for all who call themselves Americans.

To be a modern-day patriot is not so much different now than it was then. True, the world has changed much since 1776. Technology and electronic communications have given us a new appreciation for the contributions and ideologies of many races and nationalities. But being a patriot and friend to our country has never meant that we must be an enemy to the rest of mankind. Patriotism at its finest is not based on hate or bigotry; indeed, what some called patriotism is no more than unbridled mobocracy. Rather, love and faith are the building blocks of true patriotism: love—love for our fellow countrymen, to whom we are bound by common sympathies, needs, and aspirations; and faith—faith in the American ideal of democracy, an ideal that has brought happiness and prosperity to a multitude of contributing peoples and nationalities.

Being a patriot, then, is not merely a momentary thrill as the flag passes by. "I venture to suggest," observed the late Adlai Stevenson, "that patriotism is not a short and frenzied outburst of emotion but the tranquil and steady dedication of a lifetime." Regardless of our race, political preferences, or cultural traditions, we are indebted to the American patriot—and only our own patriotism can serve as repayment.

Land of the Free

The pride and faith citizens of the United States of America have in their country is particularly evident each July as flags are unfurled and fireworks puncture the evening skies. It's a time when Americans contemplate their citizenship—a citizenship many people throughout the world would be honored to share.

The founding fathers of this country believed that the most important thing in the world is a government in which freedom and liberty of the individual is protected. They believed this freedom is basic to our individual development and happiness. They also believed that each person has an obligation to serve society, to assist in the machinery that helps guarantee our freedoms.

Of course, with freedom also comes responsibility. We must try to do the right thing as we see it, but be careful not to infringe upon the freedoms of others. Since no individual is perfect, freedom may be abused. That is why we have rules in our society—because absolute freedom is anarchy, and no society can survive in such a state.

The emphasis on the rights and dignity of each person occurs again and again in our great documents. We began by declaring: "We hold these truths to be self-evident, that all men are created equal, that they are endowed by their Creator with certain inalienable Rights, that among these are Life, Liberty and the pursuit of Happiness." We live by this freedom theme and hold dearly to the sacredness and dignity of each individual. Ours is a government of the people, by the people, and for the people.

Ultimately, nations are only as strong as their ideas and people. And when citizens no longer pay attention to the first principles of a nation, the nation itself is weakened, and soon its future is in question. It is for these reasons that we welcome the pageantry and celebration that takes place each summer in thousands of cities and towns throughout this grand country. May it always be a strong and free country. And may we never take it for granted.

A Veteran

America's war veterans come in a wide variety of sizes, shapes, and ages. Their collective experience spans two world wars and several foreign conflicts. They have followed war mules through the mud of Flanders Field, dropped from landing barges onto the beaches of Normandy, faced the icy cold of Porkchop Hill, and trudged the rice paddies of the Mekong Delta. But, regardless of differences in makeup and experience, all veterans share a common bond—a brotherhood of memory and hard-won wisdom that helps define their character.

A veteran is the first man up as the flag passes by on the Fourth of July and the last man down, for he has been a witness to the blood and tears that make this and all other parades possible. A veteran is a man of peace, soft spoken, slow to anger, quick to realize that those who talk most about the glory of war are those who know least about its horror. He never jokes about war: he's been there, and still sees on memory's vivid screen the wounded and the dying, the widows and orphans; he knows first-hand that no war is good and that the only thing worse than war is slavery.

He is friend to all races of man, begrudging none; he carries with him the knowledge that it is not the man who is the enemy but enslavement and false ideologies who are the foes. Those whom he once faced across the hostile battle lines, he now esteems as his brothers. A veteran is at once proud and humble: proud of the fact that in 170 years no foreign enemy has set foot on American soil, and humble in the realization that many of his comrades who helped him make this lofty aim a reality never returned.

More than anything else, a veteran loves freedom. He can spend a whole afternoon doing nothing—just because it suits him and just because he has paid the price to do what he wants with his time. He also takes a personal pride in the freedom of others—in men and women attending the church of their choice, in friends voting how they choose, and in children sleeping quietly, without fear to interrupt their slumber.

A veteran is every man grown up a little taller—a person who understands the awesome price of life's intangibles of freedom, justice, and democracy. His motto is to live and let live. But, if he had to, if he had to choose between servitude and conflict, the veteran would once again answer a call to duty. Because, above all—above all else—a veteran is an American.

American Magnetism

Think back on it—back to the time when the only sound here in the American Rockies was the whine of wind through the lordly pines, back to when the waters of the Mississippi saw only teepee and open camps, and the rooftops of Manhattan and

Chicago were lower than her trees. Then, even then, in distant lands the word was whispered and rehearsed; the word, synonymous with hope; equivalent to liberty; more than a place—a shrine, a sanctuary for the dreams of man. Across the campfires and in the shops of Europe, behind closed doors and prison gates, with prayers and hymns, in varied tongues and accents, again and again the word was expressed: AMERICA, AMERICA.

By the thousands they came: the pioneers, the adventurers, the rejected. They carried with them their dreams, their hopes, their scant but priceless possessions—plows and seeds, lathes and anvils, sewing needles and looms—and more than that, much more: traditions and creeds, hymnals and prayer books, sacred writings in a hundred varied tongues. Think of it, the magnetism of a name, a single word: AMERICA. And the past is not alone. Observe these present years among the rice paddies and primeval forests of Southeast Asia, in boats and in dinghies, swamping in the waves of hostile seas, pressing toward this distant land of hope. Look to the south, through fences and along the waterways, for those—ever dreaming, always hoping—for the word persists: AMERICA.

This country, drawing still the discontented and disfranchised of humanity, and in each heart and on each lip rehearsed—the American catechism of law and proverb: "We, the people," "Liberty and justice for all," "In God we trust," "Help wanted," "Innocent until proven guilty," and a hundred other phrases that represent a real and daily freedom. Not perfect, not complete, ever changing and repairing—yet something still sustains the image, a basic substance, perhaps the essence of what is good in all men, distilled here from among nations in this cauldron of humanity. And thus be it ever the haven of man and the home of the free.

Goodness Leads to Greatness

More than a hundred fifty years ago when America was still an experiment, a French philosopher named Alexis de Tocqueville came to observe and report on this new land and new government.

He noted that any society needs some kind of cement to hold it together: customs, history, faith. There must be some common bond. If this bond doesn't grow naturally, it is often imposed in the form of a totalitarian government that holds people together whether they like it or not.

But here in this wide open land with a multitude of nationalities, customs, tastes, faiths, and folkways, a people had deliberately set out to leave their citizens free. The idea was exciting but terribly dangerous. De Tocqueville and others wondered what would keep this heady brew of freedom from turning every citizen into a government of his own. What would hold these scattered states together? What would keep the powerful from imposing their will on the weak if there were no strong central authority to hold them in check? Why had Americans not split already into a thousand squabbling factions? Or why had they not been locked into the iron grip of a dictator? Why were they succeeding so spectacularly?

De Tocqueville searched for the answer, and among other things he reported this, "Not until I went to the churches of America and heard her pulpits aflame with righteousness did I understand the secret of her genius and power. America is great because she is good and if America ever ceases to be good, America will cease to be great." De Tocqueville noted it was this "goodness" that bound Americans together. Not a fiery fanaticism that turned one people against another, but love, concern, and consideration of one American for another. He found a public and private acceptance that this was a nation voluntarily committing itself to the protection and guidance of God.

Of course, Americans then or now are not always good. But there was and is still in this blessed land a basic concern for other human beings and an acknowledgement of the fatherhood of God over us all. These precepts have served us well these past two centuries, and they will continue to do so. Deep down we are still committed to what Abraham Lincoln called "Firmness in the right, as God gives us to see the right." So long as we keep that commitment, America will weather the storms of the future as she has in the past.

EDUCATION

Reading—Man's Crowning Achievement

If there is one crowning achievement in the collective history of mankind, one overshadowing accomplishment from among the aggregate of human discoveries and advances, it is perhaps man's ability to read. Through that seemingly simple act, one can exchange thoughts and feelings, or transmit experience and learning, from one generation to another. Reading was once the privilege of royalty and the rich. Today, it is accessible to most of mankind. In fact, the average elementary student of today reads at higher levels than the average adult of only a few decades ago. And a short century ago, this skill was an unattainable dream for a large portion of the world's population.

The mastery, the artistry, the wonder of reading! Reading makes every person a philosopher, a poet, a statesman. Reading makes the housewife's voice as valid as that of the judge's, gives bargaining power to the coal miner and steel worker, arms citizens with the weapons to fight bureaucracy. With this single skill, more falsehoods have been uncovered, more despots dethroned, more truths enshrined than through all the battles ever fought.

They who love reading need no other gift. The mere act of reading can reduce the world to the size of a pocketbook. Through reading, we can sit in on the trial of Socrates or witness the first manned flight at Kittyhawk; we can share Robert Frost's joy in observing a tuft of flowers, peer into the souls of men with Shakespeare's piercing eyes, probe the depths of the universe with the mind of Einstein. And more. With reading we can monitor the very voice of God, through holy writ.

Reading is a key to human development. It admits us to the world of thought and imagination, to the company of saints and sages, unlocks the fetters of ignorance and superstition, and sets the soul free to muse, to venture, to experience. Yes, perhaps the mere ability to read is man's greatest achievement—the golden thread of human experience with which the poor man is made rich, and without which the richest is made poor.

The Need for Education

Once again, in most communities in this country, the learning process is underway in the schools—from kindergarten through college and on into adult education—providing a life-giving source of enrichment, not only in professional preparation, but in the overall enjoyment of life here upon the earth. We are told that "the glory of God is intelligence" (D&C 93:36), that "a wise man will hear, and will increase learning" (Prov. 1:5). This admonition applies to both the temporal and spiritual spheres. True education is the paramount purpose of a free people. It helps us develop fundamental operating principles in our lives that can guide and influence us for good. It helps make living happier by contributing to the prosperity, peace, and security of our country. So, as a free people, we must always strive for the highest and best in education.

As individuals, learning should be a lifelong endeavor . . . a continuing exercise in thinking, preparing, and living. The very process of learning helps us develop and preserve such valuable habits of the mind as curiosity, objectivity, open-mindedness, respect for evidence, and the capacity to think critically. It awakens and encourages a love of truth and contributes to our individual well-being as long as life endures. Learning need not always be a formal exercise that takes place in the classroom or in a library. Sometimes, we become educated when we least expect it. We learn through our day-to-day accomplishments, and we learn about ourselves through living. That, too, is an important part of education—learning what is inside us, finding the spark of truth that God has put into every heart, acquiring the inner knowledge of what is right and wrong for each one of us.

Some of our most vital learning takes place as we study the scriptures. We learn not only the truths of this earth, but the truth of the Creator. We learn to know him, to have confidence in him, to have faith in his laws. We learn to love him and to serve him, not because we fear him but because we have knowledge of his purpose. For most of us, the beginning of a school year is a reminder of our life-long education process, a process that includes the growth of spiritual knowledge as well as temporal learning.

A Tribute to Teachers

With autumn reappears the tradition of "back to school" for most of this nation's school students. Literally millions of youngsters once again enter an educational system that has become a model of excellence and the envy of the world. No other nation has educated its masses to the extent that this one has.

It is to American education, and more specifically to public school teachers, that we pay tribute. The success of every system or organization is dependent upon the skills and dedication of those who staff it. In education the teacher is the one who has brought America's public school system to its present successful status. To these dedicated men and women—and not all are dedicated; to those teachers who are dedicated, who man the front lines in this most important of all battles, we offer our gratitude and our respect. All who serve in the role of teacher should be held in high honor. Teachers are the allies of democracy, for only knowledge can make men free. They are the enemies of human bondage, for servitude is the product of ignorance. It is the teacher, this engineer of human character, who stands as the bridge to personal prosperity and individual achievement. As one grateful student, Lydia Sigourney, observed: "Of what unspeakable importance is [the teacher's] education who preoccupies the unwritten page of being; . . . [who] mingles with the cradle—dreams that shall be read in eternity!"

Perhaps only those who have been teachers themselves will

understand the awesome burden that our society places upon the modern-day teacher: the time spent in preparation, the ever-expanding load of paperwork, the ingratitude of some parents and students, and the problems of discipline that beset teachers daily. And perhaps only those who have taught are aware of the rewards that come to those who assist with the development of human potential. To those teachers who have raised the understanding of the world we give thanks, knowing that in spite of the educational innovations that may occur in the twenty-first century, society will never be relieved of the necessity of having sensitive and dedicated teachers.

Lifelong Learning

Every year at the beginning of summer, the nation witnesses the annual pageantry of graduation ceremonies—a time signifying the end of formal education. But the young graduates—and some are not so young—soon realize that they are, in a sense, freshmen again—that the good life is a series of learning experiences. As these newly trained people enter the professional world, they would do well to build careers on a solid foundation of steady learning and steadily developing talent. There are immense satisfactions for the individual whose job is under control. There is only anxiety for the person whose job is not.

If the school and other social institutions have done their work well, graduates will have developed habits of the mind that will be useful in new situations throughout their lives—curiosity, open-mindedness, objectivity, respect for evidence, and the capacity to think critically. If society has created an atmosphere that encourages effort, striving, and vigorous performance, the chances are that our young people will expect much of themselves.

Part of that expectation will be to continue learning. Learning must be a lifelong occupation so that there will be continual self-renewal. At the same time, there must be educational concern for the eternal man. As Spencer W. Kimball told a college faculty, "When there is an inner emptiness in the life of man, his surroundings, however affluent, cannot compensate." When there is a crisis of purpose, nothing will really seem worthwhile or meaningful. When man's relationship with God has been breached, we will be, as Isaiah said, "Like the troubled sea, when it cannot rest!" (Isa. 57:20.)

The truly educated person knows that happiness does not come from self-gratification, ease, comfort, diversion, or a state of having achieved all one's goals. Happiness involves the pursuit of meaningful goals—goals that relate the individual to a larger context of purposes, goals that call forth the full use of one's powers and talents. Graduation is, indeed, a commencement. It is a beginning toward the best that life has to offer, the foundation of which is learning, and the summit of which is true knowledge.

SELF-WORTH

The Solo and the Chorus

"If you have anything really valuable to contribute to the world," said Bruce Barton, "it will come through the expression of your own personality—that single spark of divinity that sets you off and makes you different from every other living creature." That's a compelling thought for a world where we can check best-seller lists to find out what everybody else is reading, where we can note the Nielson ratings to find out what everybody is watching, where we can look at fashion pages to see what everybody else is wearing. For many of us there's nothing safer than the invisibility and security that come from following group trends. If everybody's doing it, it must be good, it must be right, and most of all, it must be safe. Most of us would hate to do anything that *they* might criticize. What, after all, might *they* say? We live our life with our eyes continually cast over our shoulder. What Hugh B. Brown once noted still rings clear, "If any of you have a desire to be mediocre, you will probably find that you have already achieved your ambition."

Those who accomplish great things in our world, those who have moved history forward a giant step, have found that they have done so against the stings and jibes of their empty-headed critics. They have done so by responding to something deep within their own souls rather than following the superficial tugs of their world. It is easy and sometimes very pleasant to be popular. It is certainly less trying to sing with the chorus rather than venture a solo. But if we would have more than an utterly drab, uninteresting, unexplored life, we must be willing to sometimes sing our tune alone. That's what integrity is all about. The Lord did not exhaust himself with the making of two or three or four human types. He created his children with the flourish of diversity, each with his or her own genius. He expects that we will reflect his generous extravagance in our creation, that we will never be content to adopt a standard personality and suppress ourselves, no matter what the pressure. Each of us is a wonder when we have the courage to do and to be something different from the crowd.

Oh, Regard Me

To be considered important, valuable, and wanted is one of the basic needs of the human soul. Yet we're so often just a part of the crowd. At a football stadium we join thousands of indistinguishable faces, we hurry down city streets where no one recognizes us, we receive letters addressed to "occupant." It can make us wonder if our life has any distinct meaning to others. In fact, many experts think that many of our social problems stem from this human need gone astray, people searching for a way to say, "I'm important, I count for something, notice me."

The truth of the matter is we are all noticed more than we ever realize. We're noticed by friends, family, colleagues—even strangers often take notice of and are affected by things we do. But even beyond the associations with our fellowman, there is a vast amount of love and concern from him who loves us all. It should be comforting to each of us to know that the prayer of the poet, "Oh, regard me, Lord . . ." from the music "O Divine Redeemer," is answered even before it is uttered. For whether we feel praised and popular, or ignored and unknown, the Lord always regards us. To him, our importance never dims.

Jonah, the Old Testament prophet, didn't like one of the Lord's commandments to him and tried to flee from his presence. He thought of God as only a local deity from whom he could hide. Perhaps many of us also feel hidden from the Lord. Perhaps we believe, "Who am I that God should notice me?" When we remember that we are just one out of billions in the world, that perhaps our heavenward petitions must struggle for his attention, it strains our comprehension that we can be and are individually regarded by the Lord.

But we each must be assured that we are, that he does regard and love us. His attention is not focused on some cosmic mystery but on our growth. His aim is our exaltation and eternal life. His love is not limited to humanity collectively, taken as a whole and undivided. It penetrates the individual drama of a single life, to our very personal and independent existence. No, to those who know the Lord, we need not ever think we're unwanted, unloved, or unneeded. His greatest concern is our individual well-being.

Just One Person

Ours is a dependent society. In fact, we are so specialized that we depend on each other for virtually everything. Some raise the food we eat; others teach our children; our milk is delivered to us each morning by someone who depends on someone else to milk the cows. Our very survival is dependent upon others. There is, of course, value in this social reality: man is by nature a social animal, and interdependency guarantees group interaction. But there is also danger. Perhaps our modern environment of collective living has obscured the worth of the individual, the contribution just one person can make to society, and the happiness that results from self-reliance.

These days, we often hear the flimsy excuse: but I am just one man or one woman. What can I do? What was Albert Schweitzer but just one man? Yet his work relieved immeasurable suffering for the peoples of Africa and became the model for numerous medical installations in underdeveloped countries. What was Florence Nightingale but just one woman: one woman whose determination to nurse the wounded became the foundation for the present-day Red Cross.

Single individuals have altered the course of world history. The words "We shall never surrender" were spoken by one man in the dark days prior to World War II, when the survival of the free world was in doubt—words from Winston Churchill, who became the living symbol of defiance to the advancing war machines. History has proven that the value and strength of society depend less on what men have in common than upon what men hold apart. In truth, where uniformity has been the rule, stagnation has been the result.

We march too often in platoons. Our individuality is enslaved by fads and fashions, is bought and sold by the auctioneers of the daily marketplace, lies spoiled by the decaying forces of social pressure, and bows before the false god of uniformity. Every identity has his or her own beauty—sublime uniqueness that is the essence of individuality—and every person has a personal contribution to make that he alone can offer—to neighbors, to society, and to the world.

Know Thyself

Above the entrance to the ancient Greek shrine at Delphi were inscribed these two words: "Know Thyself." The message contained in this short injunction still merits our consideration. For while science has given us the telescope to scan the far reaches of the stellar universe and the microscope to probe the unseen microcosms, the greatest frontier continues to be the uncharted regions of self.

In truth, a full understanding of the universe that surrounds us is unattainable without first knowing ourselves. It is from this personal vantage point that all other spheres are observed and understood. To a large extent, all of the value judgments we make are a product of what we think we have become. Our political preferences, the automobile we drive, what we think is beautiful, and sometimes even our religious persuasions are a result of our past environment and experience. To know ourselves is to understand the reasons behind our likes and dislikes, our preferences and aversions.

Thus, in learning about ourselves we also learn about others. When we understand that what we are is dependent in measure upon what we have been, we become more tolerant of what others are; we begin to see that our experience has been the same as others, and our conclusions may have also been the same as others. We become aware that bigotry, racial hatred, and international disputes are not based as much in ignorance of other people as they are in ignorance of ourselves. Perhaps, had we sought to understand ourselves before we judged others, the annals of humanity would have been a history of peace rather than a chronicle of war.

The application of this ancient maxim lies within the grasp of all who take the time and expend the energy to truly know themselves: to understand their skills and aptitudes, their weaknesses and strengths; to measure the distance between where they are and where they want to be. To "know thyself," we must explore our feelings about the world, about politics, religion, social issues; we must attempt to see ourselves as others see us. Finally, to "know thyself" as only God can know us, we must search inwardly for the innate and unique gifts that lie within every individual and, once found, nurture and develop them. Perhaps then we might begin to understand the meaning of the words "Know Thyself."

Illusions

One of the realities of this life is that everything is not as it appears; or more appropriately, everything is not as we perceive it. We filter what we see through our own imaginations, our own sentiments, through our own values and aspirations. We see, as Paul the apostle noted, "through a glass, darkly" (1 Cor. 13:12), perceiving illusions as reality and at times reality as illusion.

The reasons for the existence of illusions are varied and complex, but a contributing factor lies within ourselves, with our desire to appear to be something we are not. Because of our own insecurities, we foster illusions. The poor would appear rich; the ignorant would seem wise; youth would present itself as age, while age would portray the image of youth. Perhaps our psychological survival depends upon the existence of illusions, or perhaps the psyche is not equipped to see ourselves as we are, or others as they are. But more likely, our survival and ultimate success as individuals is directly proportional to our ability to see through our own illusions and the appearances of others.

In marriage, it is not the couple who continue to hide behind the romantic but false images of infatuation who survive. Rather the enduring relationship grows upon the personal realities of each partner's strengths and weaknesses—a relationship devoid of false images and fanciful expectations. Parents also need to practice objectivity when viewing their children. Certainly, we parents have been and will continue to be idealistic about our children. But to project unattainable goals on our children because we see them as being more gifted than they are—or to distort their own self-images by refusing to acknowledge their weaknesses—is harmful to both parent and child.

For individuals, it is imperative that we not only see ourselves as we are, but that we accept these real reflections of ourselves. Insanity is nothing more than the conquest of reality by illusion. Sooner or later that individual who cannot or will not accept himself for what he is, jeopardizes personal well-being. To walk without illusion, to care more about inner worth than outward appearances, to project no other images beyond our own characters, to be what we are—these are the marks of an individual at peace with himself.

Identity

There is a question that haunts every human being—"Who am I?" Sometimes it wears other faces, such as "Am I competent? Am I loved? Am I worthwhile?" Rarely does it disappear altogether. It is a question we each ask as life brings us our varied situations.

In that ongoing struggle to find ourselves and to feel good about what we find, we are likely to make some mistakes. One is to define ourselves solely by what we do, because what we do is as transient as the wind, as life forces unsuspected changes on us. One day we are children, the next day adults. One day we have a certain job, the next day technology has rendered it obsolete. One day we can handle a task competently, the next day illness or increased responsibilities make us lose control. Others of us jeopardize our identity by basing it on how others respond to us. We stand vulnerable and afraid upon life's stages, waiting for applause; and if it doesn't come, we are crushed and broken. "I am only who you think I am," we say with pleading eyes, the center of our lives in the careless hands of others.

Discovering who we are, by our own definition, may be life's most important task. Vincent Van Gogh said, "Sometimes I feel more like myself." Feeling more like ourselves may be the best safeguard against misery. Nothing is more painful than feeling lost, doubting our abilities, being at the mercy of another's view of us. That is Satan's best tool against us, and it is the same tool he tried to use against the Savior when Christ had been fasting forty days upon the mount. How subtle for Satan to suggest to him, "If thou be the Son of God, command that these stones be made bread." (Matt. 4:3.) That taunting "if." The temptation was not just to his hunger. Far more it was to his identity, to make him doubt that he was the Son of God.

The same tool is used to defeat us. We hear, "If you are worthwhile . . ." "If you are a good person . . ." "If you are who you think you are . . ." But we can defeat that taunting "if," and the best place to do it is on our knees, the Lord revealing to us who we are and always have been. We are myopic, caught here in the darkness of mortality, but he can see. And his view is the long view. "Who am I?" we ask, and the world gives mixed answers. But the Lord will affirm that we are each different and each, like the rest of his creation, "good."

Appendix

The following is an alphabetical listing of all titles contained in A *Time for Reflection* and their corresponding broadcast dates.

After the Death of a Loved One, October 17, 1982
American Family—An Endangered Species, The, August 9, 1981
American Magnetism, July 1, 1984
Anxious Living, January 24, 1982
Appearance and Reality, September 14, 1980
Art of Staying Young, The, November 6, 1983
Autumn's Special Message, September 28, 1980
Back to the Basics, October 5, 1980
Being a Patriot, July 5, 1981
Best of Life, The, June 17, 1984
Blessing of Freedom, The, August 7, 1983
Building Strong Families, December 5, 1982
By Faith All Things Are Possible, January 13, 1985
Choosing Good, June 24, 1984
Come, February 20, 1983
Coming, The, December 19, 1982
Day for Reflection, A, May 27, 1984
Defeating Discouragement, January 22, 1984
Discipline Brings Freedom, August 5, 1984
Do We Despise Him?, April 15, 1984
Enemy is Fear, The, May 4, 1980
Eternal Value of Virtuous Living, The, March 4, 1984
Facing Problems, February 10, 1985
Faith, November 13, 1983
Faith in God, March 13, 1983

Index

Dostoyevski, Fyodor, 60
Duty, 71-72

Easter, 123-24
Education: of children, 91-92;
    importance of, 170-73
Electricity, example of, 61
Embroidery, intellectual, 5
Emotional storms, 3-4
Enjoyment of life, 4-5
Epictetus, 30
Eros, 68
Eternal laws, 17, 41
Eternal progression, 3-4
Evans, Richard L., 140
Evil and good, choosing between,
    35-36, 102-3
Existential Voyage, 4-5
Experience, learning lessons from,
    42-43
Extinction, fear of, 123

Failure, success and, 27-30
Faith: in self, 25-26; development of,
    47-48; decline of, 48-50; science
    and, 52-53
False happiness, 17
Families as foundation of society, 80,
    83-88
Fathers, influence of, 92-94
Fear: and faith, 51-52; of extinction,
    123
Fellowman, service to, 101-2, 105-6,
    125
Fleischer, Leon, 44
Forefathers, responsibility to,
    157-58, 162
Forgiveness, 108-9
Franklin, Benjamin, 7
Freedom: of Christ, 15; and
    self-discipline, 28-29; foundations
    of, 157-58; blessings of, 158-59;
    of pioneers, 159-60; of individuals,
    161-62; veterans love of, 162-63
Friendship, 15
Fuel, spiritual, 107-8
Fulfillment, autumn as season of,
    135-36
Fun, happiness is more than, 18-19

Gehrig, Lou, 24
Gift, prayer is a, 61-62
Gloominess, 16
God: nature of, 11-18; relationships
    with, 14; peace comes from, 36;
    faith in, 48-49; dependence upon,
    57-58, 106; communication with,
    59-60; love of, 70-71, 73-74,
    178-79; duty toward, 71-72;
    handiwork of, 134-35, 178; truth
    about, 171
Good and evil, choosing between,
    35-36, 102-3
Good Samaritan, 106
Goodness of Americans, 164-65
Gospel, happiness and the, 18

Habits, 5
Happiness: not found in material
    things, 4, 7, 13; religion and,
    13-14; not found in selfishness,
    16-17; of God, 18; pursuit of, 19;
    in marriage, 81-82
Harmony, loss of inner, 9
Henry, Patrick, 157
Heroes, unsung, 24
Holmes, Oliver Wendell, 144

Identity, personal, 182-83
Illusions, 181-82
Imitation of Christ, 108, 152
Independence, 57-58
Individuality, 177-78, 180
Inner harmony, loss of, 9
Integrity, 177-78
Intellectual embroidery, 5

"Jesu, Joy of Man's Desiring," 14
Jesus Christ: joy in life of, 14-15;
    atonement of, 32; calms sea, 35;
    as example of love, 69, 72-73; as
    example of forgiveness, 108-9;
    resurrection of, 114-15, 124; as
    foundation, 115-16; birth of,
    117-18, 125-27; sorrow of,
    118-19; identity of, 183
"Jesus the Very Thought of Thee,"
    107

Joy, 14-15
Judgment Day, 130

Kimball, Spencer W., 172-73
Kingdom of Christ, 114-15
"Know Thyself," 180-81

Laughter, success and, 23-24
Laws, eternal, 41
Leisure, 18, 23
Lewis, C. S., 106, 132
Liberty. *See* Freedom
Life: enjoyment of, 4-5; simplification of, 5-9, 23; distractions of, 8-9; storms in, 15; setting priorities in, 23; problems are a condition of, 36-37; sadness is a part of, 40
Lincoln, Abraham, 165
"Lord is my Shepherd," 50
Lord's prayer, 63
Love: definition of, 68-71, 74-75; of God, 70-71, 73-74, 178-79; of mothers, 93-98; of country, 161
Luck, success and, 30-31

MacArthur, Douglas, 93
Man: who gets caught in blizzard, 58; who sees nothing in painting, 128
Marriage, 79-82, 182
Massachetts, Plymouth, 128
Maxwell, Neal A., 5
McKay, David O., 152
"Me" society, 16-17
Mediocrity, 177
Memorial Day, 129
Mere Christianity, 106
Moral courage, 25-26
Mother who visits son in prison, 97-98
Mothers, influence of, 93-98
Movement, religious, 14
Myths of aging, 152-53

Nature: self-renewal of, 3; happiness found in, 19; beauty of, 130-31; reawakening of, 133-35
Needs, simplification of, 5-9
New Year's Day, 13

New York Yankees, 24
Nielson ratings, 177
Nineteenth-century home, 82-83

Opportunities, difficulties can become, 27, 30
Optimism, 151-52

Parenthood, responsibilities of, 91-92
Patriotism, 160-61
Peace, God-given, 36
Perfection, laws of, 107
Persistence, 29
Personal identity, 182-83
Pessimism, 19
Philios, 69
Philosopher who visits America, 164-65
Physical storms, 3-4
Pianist who loses control of fingers, 44
Pioneers, 159-60
Pleasure, pursuit of, 17
Plymouth, Massachusetts, 128
Positive thinking, 50
Power: of faith, 49-50; of prayer, 60-61
Prayer, importance of, 57-63
Priorities, 23, 84-85
Problems, overcoming, 36-37, 41-42
Process of faith, 49-51
Professional titles, success and, 23
Progression, eternal, 3-4
Prophets, faith shown by, 47-48
Punishment, 41

Qualities of service, 101-2

Reading, importance of, 169-70
Reality and appearance, 142-43, 181-82
Recreation, 23
Religion and happiness, 13-14
Repetitions, vain, 63
Responsibility to forefathers, 157-58, 162
Resurrection of Christ, 114-15, 124
Role of religion, 13-14
Roosevelt, Eleanor, 42